6th Grade

MARYLAND

MATH
TEST
PREP

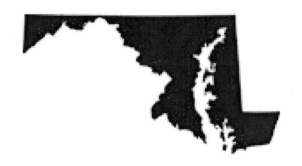

Common Core
State Standards

Our 6th Grade Math Test Prep for Common Core State Standards is an excellent resource to supplement your classroom's curriculum to assess and manage students' understanding of concepts outlined in the Common Core State Standards Initiative. This resource is divided into three sections: Diagnostic, Practice, and Assessment with multiple choice questions in each section. We recommend you use the Diagnostic section as a tool to determine the students' areas that need to be retaught. We also recommend you encourage your students to show their work to determine *how* and *why* the student arrived at an answer. The Practice section should be used to strengthen the students' knowledge by re-testing the standard to ensure comprehension of each standard. To ensure students' apply taught concepts in the classroom, we advise you use the Assessment section as a final test to verify the students' have mastered the standard.

This resource contains over 1000 practice problems aligned to the Common Core State Standards. To view the standards, refer to pages *i* through *viii*.

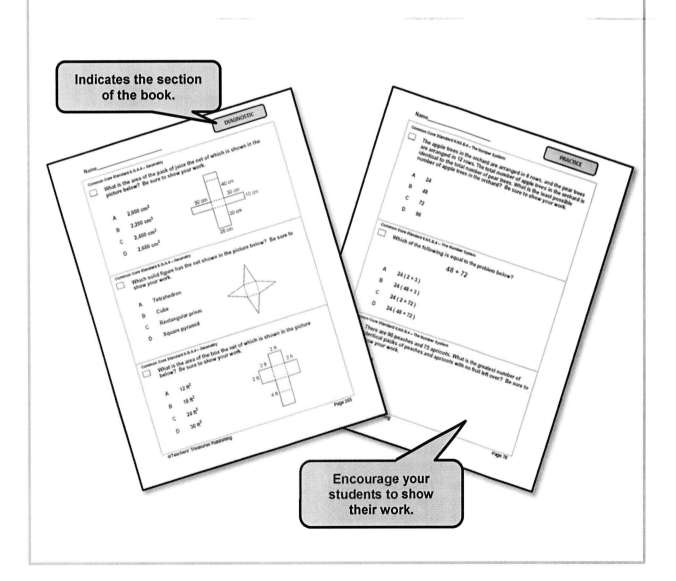

Indicates the section of the book.

Encourage your students to show their work.

6th Grade
Math Test Prep
FOR
Common Core
Standards

Ratios & Proportional Relationships   6.RP

Understand ratio concepts and use ratio reasoning to solve problems.

CCSS.MATH.CONTENT.6.RP.A.1
Understand the concept of a ratio and use ratio language to describe a ratio relationship between two quantities. *For example, "The ratio of wings to beaks in the bird house at the zoo was 2:1, because for every 2 wings there was 1 beak." "For every vote candidate A received, candidate C received nearly three votes."*

CCSS.MATH.CONTENT.6.RP.A.2
Understand the concept of a unit rate a/b associated with a ratio a:b with b ≠ 0, and use rate language in the context of a ratio relationship. *For example, "This recipe has a ratio of 3 cups of flour to 4 cups of sugar, so there is 3/4 cup of flour for each cup of sugar." "We paid $75 for 15 hamburgers, which is a rate of $5 per hamburger."*

CCSS.MATH.CONTENT.6.RP.A.3
Use ratio and rate reasoning to solve real-world and mathematical problems, e.g., by reasoning about tables of equivalent ratios, tape diagrams, double number line diagrams, or equations.

CCSS.MATH.CONTENT.6.RP.A.3.A
Make tables of equivalent ratios relating quantities with whole-number measurements, find missing values in the tables, and plot the pairs of values on the coordinate plane. Use tables to compare ratios.

CCSS.MATH.CONTENT.6.RP.A.3.B
Solve unit rate problems including those involving unit pricing and constant speed. *For example, if it took 7 hours to mow 4 lawns, then at that rate, how many lawns could be mowed in 35 hours? At what rate were lawns being mowed?*

CCSS.MATH.CONTENT.6.RP.A.3.C
Find a percent of a quantity as a rate per 100 (e.g., 30% of a quantity means 30/100 times the quantity); solve problems involving finding the whole, given a part and the percent.

CCSS.MATH.CONTENT.6.RP.A.3.D
Use ratio reasoning to convert measurement units; manipulate and transform units appropriately when multiplying or dividing quantities.

The Number System 6.NS

Apply and extend previous understandings of multiplication and division to divide fractions by fractions.

CCSS.MATH.CONTENT.6.NS.A.1
Interpret and compute quotients of fractions, and solve word problems involving division of fractions by fractions, e.g., by using visual fraction models and equations to represent the problem. *For example, create a story context for (2/3) ÷ (3/4) and use a visual fraction model to show the quotient; use the relationship between multiplication and division to explain that (2/3) ÷ (3/4) = 8/9 because 3/4 of 8/9 is 2/3. (In general, (a/b) ÷ (c/d) = ad/bc.) How much chocolate will each person get if 3 people share 1/2 lb of chocolate equally? How many 3/4-cup servings are in 2/3 of a cup of yogurt? How wide is a rectangular strip of land with length 3/4 mi and area 1/2 square mi?*.

Compute fluently with multi-digit numbers and find common factors and multiples.

CCSS.MATH.CONTENT.6.NS.B.2
Fluently divide multi-digit numbers using the standard algorithm.

CCSS.MATH.CONTENT.6.NS.B.3
Fluently add, subtract, multiply, and divide multi-digit decimals using the standard algorithm for each operation.

CCSS.MATH.CONTENT.6.NS.B.4
Find the greatest common factor of two whole numbers less than or equal to 100 and the least common multiple of two whole numbers less than or equal to 12. Use the distributive property to express a sum of two whole numbers 1-100 with a common factor as a multiple of a sum of two whole numbers with no common factor. *For example, express 36 + 8 as 4 (9 + 2).*

Apply and extend previous understandings of numbers to the system of rational numbers.

CCSS.MATH.CONTENT.6.NS.C.5
Understand that positive and negative numbers are used together to describe quantities having opposite directions or values (e.g., temperature above/below zero, elevation above/below sea level, credits/debits, positive/negative electric charge); use positive and negative numbers to represent quantities in real-world contexts, explaining the meaning of 0 in each situation.

CCSS.MATH.CONTENT.6.NS.C.6

Understand a rational number as a point on the number line. Extend number line diagrams and coordinate axes familiar from previous grades to represent points on the line and in the plane with negative number coordinates.

CCSS.MATH.CONTENT.6.NS.C.6.A

Recognize opposite signs of numbers as indicating locations on opposite sides of 0 on the number line; recognize that the opposite of the opposite of a number is the number itself, e.g., -(-3) = 3, and that 0 is its own opposite.

CCSS.MATH.CONTENT.6.NS.C.6.B

Understand signs of numbers in ordered pairs as indicating locations in quadrants of the coordinate plane; recognize that when two ordered pairs differ only by signs, the locations of the points are related by reflections across one or both axes.

CCSS.MATH.CONTENT.6.NS.C.6.C

Find and position integers and other rational numbers on a horizontal or vertical number line diagram; find and position pairs of integers and other rational numbers on a coordinate plane.

CCSS.MATH.CONTENT.6.NS.C.7

Understand ordering and absolute value of rational numbers.

CCSS.MATH.CONTENT.6.NS.C.7.A

Interpret statements of inequality as statements about the relative position of two numbers on a number line diagram. *For example, interpret -3 > -7 as a statement that -3 is located to the right of -7 on a number line oriented from left to right.*

CCSS.MATH.CONTENT.6.NS.C.7.B

Write, interpret, and explain statements of order for rational numbers in real-world contexts. *For example, write -3 °C > -7 °C to express the fact that -3 °C is warmer than -7 °C.*

CCSS.MATH.CONTENT.6.NS.C.7.C

Understand the absolute value of a rational number as its distance from 0 on the number line; interpret absolute value as magnitude for a positive or negative quantity in a real-world situation. *For example, for an account balance of -30 dollars, write |-30| = 30 to describe the size of the debt in dollars.*

CCSS.MATH.CONTENT.6.NS.C.7.D
Distinguish comparisons of absolute value from statements about order. *For example, recognize that an account balance less than -30 dollars represents a debt greater than 30 dollars.*

CCSS.MATH.CONTENT.6.NS.C.8
Solve real-world and mathematical problems by graphing points in all four quadrants of the coordinate plane. Include use of coordinates and absolute value to find distances between points with the same first coordinate or the same second coordinate.

Expressions & Equations   6.EE

Apply and extend previous understandings of arithmetic to algebraic expressions.

CCSS.MATH.CONTENT.6.EE.A.1
Write and evaluate numerical expressions involving whole-number exponents.

CCSS.MATH.CONTENT.6.EE.A.2
Write, read, and evaluate expressions in which letters stand for numbers.

CCSS.MATH.CONTENT.6.EE.A.2.A
Write expressions that record operations with numbers and with letters standing for numbers. *For example, express the calculation "Subtract y from 5" as 5 - y.*

CCSS.MATH.CONTENT.6.EE.A.2.B
Identify parts of an expression using mathematical terms (sum, term, product, factor, quotient, coefficient); view one or more parts of an expression as a single entity. *For example, describe the expression 2 (8 + 7) as a product of two factors; view (8 + 7) as both a single entity and a sum of two terms.*

CCSS.MATH.CONTENT.6.EE.A.2.C
Evaluate expressions at specific values of their variables. Include expressions that arise from formulas used in real-world problems. Perform arithmetic operations, including those involving whole-number exponents, in the

conventional order when there are no parentheses to specify a particular order (Order of Operations). *For example, use the formulas $V = s^3$ and $A = 6 s^2$ to find the volume and surface area of a cube with sides of length s = 1/2.*

CCSS.MATH.CONTENT.6.EE.A.3

Apply the properties of operations to generate equivalent expressions. *For example, apply the distributive property to the expression 3 (2 + x) to produce the equivalent expression 6 + 3x; apply the distributive property to the expression 24x + 18y to produce the equivalent expression 6 (4x + 3y); apply properties of operations to y + y + y to produce the equivalent expression 3y.*

CCSS.MATH.CONTENT.6.EE.A.4

Identify when two expressions are equivalent (i.e., when the two expressions name the same number regardless of which value is substituted into them). *For example, the expressions y + y + y and 3y are equivalent because they name the same number regardless of which number y stands for.*

Reason about and solve one-variable equations and inequalities.

CCSS.MATH.CONTENT.6.EE.B.5

Understand solving an equation or inequality as a process of answering a question: which values from a specified set, if any, make the equation or inequality true? Use substitution to determine whether a given number in a specified set makes an equation or inequality true.

CCSS.MATH.CONTENT.6.EE.B.6

Use variables to represent numbers and write expressions when solving a real-world or mathematical problem; understand that a variable can represent an unknown number, or, depending on the purpose at hand, any number in a specified set.

CCSS.MATH.CONTENT.6.EE.B.7

Solve real-world and mathematical problems by writing and solving equations of the form $x + p = q$ and $px = q$ for cases in which p, q and x are all nonnegative rational numbers.

CCSS.MATH.CONTENT.6.EE.B.8

Write an inequality of the form $x > c$ or $x < c$ to represent a constraint or condition in a real-world or mathematical problem. Recognize that inequalities of the form $x > c$ or $x <$

c have infinitely many solutions; represent solutions of such inequalities on number line diagrams.

Represent and analyze quantitative relationships between dependent and independent variables.

CCSS.MATH.CONTENT.6.EE.C.9
Use variables to represent two quantities in a real-world problem that change in relationship to one another; write an equation to express one quantity, thought of as the dependent variable, in terms of the other quantity, thought of as the independent variable. Analyze the relationship between the dependent and independent variables using graphs and tables, and relate these to the equation. For example, in a problem involving motion at constant speed, list and graph ordered pairs of distances and times, and write the equation d = 65t to represent the relationship between distance and time.

Geometry   6.G

Solve real-world and mathematical problems involving area, surface area, and volume.

CCSS.MATH.CONTENT.6.G.A.1
Find the area of right triangles, other triangles, special quadrilaterals, and polygons by composing into rectangles or decomposing into triangles and other shapes; apply these techniques in the context of solving real-world and mathematical problems.

CCSS.MATH.CONTENT.6.G.A.2
Find the volume of a right rectangular prism with fractional edge lengths by packing it with unit cubes of the appropriate unit fraction edge lengths, and show that the volume is the same as would be found by multiplying the edge lengths of the prism. Apply the formulas $V = l\,w\,h$ and $V = b\,h$ to find volumes of right rectangular prisms with fractional edge lengths in the context of solving real-world and mathematical problems.

CCSS.MATH.CONTENT.6.G.A.3
Draw polygons in the coordinate plane given coordinates for the vertices; use coordinates to find the length of a side joining points with the same first coordinate or the same second coordinate. Apply these techniques in the context of solving real-world and mathematical problems.

CCSS.MATH.CONTENT.6.G.A.4
Represent three-dimensional figures using nets made up of rectangles and triangles,

and use the nets to find the surface area of these figures. Apply these techniques in the context of solving real-world and mathematical problems.

Statistics & Probability   6.SP

Develop understanding of statistical variability.

CCSS.MATH.CONTENT.6.SP.A.1
Recognize a statistical question as one that anticipates variability in the data related to the question and accounts for it in the answers. *For example, "How old am I?" is not a statistical question, but "How old are the students in my school?" is a statistical question because one anticipates variability in students' ages.*

CCSS.MATH.CONTENT.6.SP.A.2
Understand that a set of data collected to answer a statistical question has a distribution which can be described by its center, spread, and overall shape.

CCSS.MATH.CONTENT.6.SP.A.3
Recognize that a measure of center for a numerical data set summarizes all of its values with a single number, while a measure of variation describes how its values vary with a single number.

Summarize and describe distributions.

CCSS.MATH.CONTENT.6.SP.B.4
Display numerical data in plots on a number line, including dot plots, histograms, and box plots.

CCSS.MATH.CONTENT.6.SP.B.5
Summarize numerical data sets in relation to their context, such as by:

CCSS.MATH.CONTENT.6.SP.B.5.A
Reporting the number of observations.

CCSS.MATH.CONTENT.6.SP.B.5.B
Describing the nature of the attribute under investigation, including how it was measured and its units of measurement.

CCSS.MATH.CONTENT.6.SP.B.5.C

Giving quantitative measures of center (median and/or mean) and variability (interquartile range and/or mean absolute deviation), as well as describing any overall pattern and any striking deviations from the overall pattern with reference to the context in which the data were gathered.

CCSS.MATH.CONTENT.6.SP.B.5.D

Relating the choice of measures of center and variability to the shape of the data distribution and the context in which the data were gathered.

LENGTH

Metric

1 kilometer = 1000 meters
1 meter = 100 centimeters
1 centimeter = 10 millimeters

Customary

1 yard = 3 feet
1 foot = 12 inches

CAPACITY & VOLUME

Metric

1 liter = 1000 milliliters

Customary

1 gallon = 4 quarts
1 gallon = 128 ounces
1 quart = 2 pints
1 pint = 2 cups
1 cup = 8 ounces

MASS & WEIGHT

Metric

1 kilogram = 1000 grams
1 gram = 1000 milligrams

Customary

1 ton = 2000 pounds
1 pound = 16 ounces

TIME

1 year = 365 days

1 year = 12 months

1 year = 52 weeks

1 week = 7 days

1 day = 24 hours

1 hour = 60 minutes

1 minute = 60 seconds

MATHEMATICS CHART

Perimeter	square	$P = 4s$
	rectangle	$P = 2l + 2w$ or $P = 2(l + w)$

Circumference	circle	$C = 2\pi r$ or $C = \pi d$

Area	square	$A = s^2$
	rectangle	$A = lw$ or $A = bh$
	triangle	$A = \frac{1}{2}bh$ or $A = \frac{bh}{2}$
	trapezoid	$A = \frac{1}{2}(b_1 + b_2)h$ or $A = \frac{(b_1 + b_2)h}{2}$
	circle	$A = \pi r^2$

Volume	cube	$V = s^3$
	rectangular prism	$V = lwh$

Pi	π	$\pi \approx 3.14$ or $\pi \approx \frac{22}{7}$

Name_____

Common Core Standard 6.RP.A.1 – Ratios & Proportional Relationships

☐ **For every 3 women at the local shoe store there are 2 men. What is the possible number of women and men in the store? Be sure to show your work.**

A   9 women, 4 men

B   4 women, 9 men

C   9 women, 6 men

D   6 women, 9 men

Common Core Standard 6.RP.A.1 – Ratios & Proportional Relationships

☐ **What is the ratio of circles to squares in the picture below? Be sure to show your work.**

A   3 to 2

B   2 to 3

C   3 to 5

D   2 to 5

Common Core Standard 6.RP.A.1 – Ratios & Proportional Relationships

☐ **There are 16 boys and 8 girls in the class. What is the ratio of girls to boys? Be sure to show your work.**

A   2:1

B   1:2

C   2:3

D   1:3

Name_____

Common Core Standard 6.RP.A.1 – Ratios & Proportional Relationships

☐ There were 12 rainy days in the month of April. What was the ratio of rainy days to clear days in April? Be sure to show your work.

A   2:5

B   5:2

C   2:3

D   3:2

Common Core Standard 6.RP.A.1 – Ratios & Proportional Relationships

☐ What is the ratio of dogs to all animals in the picture below? Be sure to show your work.

A   4:5

B   2:1

C   1:2

D   1:5

Common Core Standard 6.RP.A.1 – Ratios & Proportional Relationships

☐ Tyler collects stamps. He has 8 stamps from XIX century and 12 stamps from XX century. What is the ratio of stamps from XIX century to all stamps in Tyler's collection? Be sure to show your work.

A   3 to 2

B   2 to 3

C   5 to 2

D   2 to 5

Common Core Standard 6.RP.A.1 – Ratios & Proportional Relationships

☐ Samantha found bottles of water and soda in the basement. The ratio of bottles of water to all bottles is 1:3. What is the possible number of bottles of water and soda in the basement? Be sure to show your work.

A   10 bottles of water, 30 bottles of soda

B   15 bottles of water, 5 bottles of soda

C   10 bottles of water, 20 bottles of soda

D   10 bottles of water, 5 bottles of soda

Common Core Standard 6.RP.A.1 – Ratios & Proportional Relationships

☐ What is the ratio of glasses to bottles in the picture below? Be sure to show your work.

A   3 to 1

B   3 to 2

C   1 to 2

D   2 to 1

Common Core Standard 6.RP.A.1 – Ratios & Proportional Relationships

☐ Michael is 4 ft. tall and his father is 6 ft. tall. What is the ratio of Michael's height to his father's height? Be sure to show your work.

A   2:3

B   3:2

C   2:5

D   3:5

Name_____

Common Core Standard 6.RP.A.1 – Ratios & Proportional Relationships

☐ The length of the swimming pool is 100 m, and its width is 50 m. What is the ratio of width to length of the swimming pool? Be sure to show your work.

A   2 to 1

B   1 to 2

C   2 to 3

D   1 to 3

Common Core Standard 6.RP.A.1 – Ratios & Proportional Relationships

☐ What is the ratio of boys to girls in the picture below? Be sure to show your work.

A   1:2

B   2:1

C   2:3

D   1:1

Common Core Standard 6.RP.A.1 – Ratios & Proportional Relationships

☐ For every 7 days in a week Emily rides a bicycle 3 days. What is the ratio of days when Emily rides a bicycle to the days when Emily doesn't ride a bicycle? Be sure to show your work.

A   3:7

B   4:7

C   3:4

D   4:3

Name_____

Common Core Standard 6.RP.A.1 – Ratios & Proportional Relationships

☐ **Logan and Emma are candidates at the school election. For every 6 student voters, 2 of them voted for Logan. What is the possible number of students who voted for Logan and Emma? Be sure to show your work.**

A   120 for Logan, 240 for Emma

B   120 for Logan, 360 for Emma

C   120 for Emma, 240 for Logan

D   120 for Emma, 360 for Logan

Common Core Standard 6.RP.A.1 – Ratios & Proportional Relationships

☐ **Look at the bottles of soda in the picture below, both are proportional in size. What is the ratio of their heights? Be sure to show your work.**

A   2 to 3

B   2 to 5

C   3 to 5

D   5 to 6

12 cm  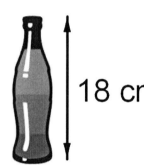 18 cm

Common Core Standard 6.RP.A.1 – Ratios & Proportional Relationships

☐ **Mia has 36 forks and 24 knives in her silverware drawer. What is the ratio of knives to forks in the drawer? Be sure to show your work.**

A   3:2

B   2:3

C   3:5

D   2:5

Name_____

Common Core Standard 6.RP.A.1 – Ratios & Proportional Relationships

☐ There are 50 empty seats on the bus, and 20 passengers. What is the ratio of passengers to empty seats? Be sure to show your work.

A   2:5

B   3:5

C   2:3

D   3:2

Common Core Standard 6.RP.A.1 – Ratios & Proportional Relationships

☐ Look at the spiral notebooks in the picture, both are proportional in size. What is the ratio of their heights? Be sure to show your work.

A   3 to 1

B   3 to 4

C   2 to 1

D   2 to 3

18 cm     24 cm

Common Core Standard 6.RP.A.1 – Ratios & Proportional Relationships

☐ The perimeters of two squares are 16 in. and 20 in. What is the ratio of the lengths of their sides? Be sure to show your work.

A   5 to 9

B   4 to 9

C   5 to 6

D   4 to 5

Common Core Standard 6.RP.A.1 – Ratios & Proportional Relationships

☐ **For every 6 employed workers there are 2 uneployed. What is the possible number of employed and unemployed workers? Be sure to show your work.**

A   300 employed, 100 unemployed

B   400 employed, 100 unemployed

C   100 employed, 300 unemployed

D   100 employed, 400 unemployed

Common Core Standard 6.RP.A.1 – Ratios & Proportional Relationships

☐ **Look at the toy cars in the picture below, both are proportional in size. What is the ratio of their lengths? Be sure to show your work.**

A   2 to 1

B   1 to 3

C   3 to 1

D   3 to 2

18 cm   12 cm

Common Core Standard 6.RP.A.1 – Ratios & Proportional Relationships

☐ **There are 12 Americans, 8 Italians, and 10 Germans in an international science team competition. What is the ratio of Italians to Americans? Be sure to show your work.**

A   3:2

B   3:5

C   2:3

D   2:5

Common Core Standard 6.RP.A.1 – Ratios & Proportional Relationships

☐ **Carollton High School football team has 24 juniors and 36 seniors. What is the ratio of juniors to seniors? Be sure to show your work.**

A   1 to 2

B   2 to 3

C   3 to 4

D   3 to 5

Common Core Standard 6.RP.A.1 – Ratios & Proportional Relationships

☐ **Look at the dolls in the picture below, both are proportional in size. What is the ratio of their heights? Be sure to show your work.**

A   1:2

B   2:3

C   3:4

D   4:5

12 in   15 in

Common Core Standard 6.RP.A.1 – Ratios & Proportional Relationships

☐ **The ratio of employees at Mica's mother's company of white collar workers to blue collar workers is 2 to 5. What is the possible number of high skilled and non qualified workers? Be sure to show your work.**

A   80 white collar, 200 blue collar

B   100 white collar, 40 blue collar

C   250 white collar, 100 blue collar

D   60 white collar, 210 blue collar

Common Core Standard 6.RP.A.2 – Ratios & Proportional Relationships

☐ **Emma's mother bought Emma 12 pairs of socks for $72. What is the price of one pair of socks? Be sure to show your work.**

A $6

B $12

C $60

D $84

Common Core Standard 6.RP.A.2 – Ratios & Proportional Relationships

☐ **Fill in the missing number in the statement below. Be sure to show your work.**

84 miles in 14 days = _____ miles per day

A   5

B   6

C   7

D   8

Common Core Standard 6.RP.A.2 – Ratios & Proportional Relationships

☐ **Joshua's literature homework assignment is to read a book that has 96 total pages. If Joshua reads 12 pages each day, how many days will it take him to finish the book? Be sure to show your work.**

A   6

B   7

C   8

D   9

Common Core Standard 6.RP.A.2 – Ratios & Proportional Relationships

☐ Hannah sold 48 flowers in 3 hours at the farmer's market. If she continues to sells at that rate, how many flowers will she sell in the next 2 hours? Be sure to show your work.

A   4

B   8

C   16

D   32

Common Core Standard 6.RP.A.2 – Ratios & Proportional Relationships

☐ Fill in the missing number in the statement below. Be sure to show your work.

75 students in ____ classrooms = 25 students per classroom

A   2

B   3

C   4

D   5

Common Core Standard 6.RP.A.2 – Ratios & Proportional Relationships

☐ Joseph went to visit his grandmother with his parents. They drove 240 miles in 4 hours. What was the average speed they were traveling?   Be sure to show your work.

A   40 miles per hour

B   55 miles per hour

C   60 miles per hour

D   65 miles per hour

Common Core Standard 6.RP.A.2 – Ratios & Proportional Relationships

☐ **Olivia had 24 guests at her birthday party last year, which bought 18 liters of juice for her guests. This year she is expecting 40 guests. How many liters of juice does she need to buy for a birthday party this year? Be sure to show your work.**

A 18 liters

B 24 liters

C 30 liters

D 32 liters

Common Core Standard 6.RP.A.2 – Ratios & Proportional Relationships

☐ **Fill in the missing number in the statement below. Be sure to show your work.**

____ birds in 12 cages = 4 birds per cage

A 8

B 16

C 24

D 48

Common Core Standard 6.RP.A.2 – Ratios & Proportional Relationships

☐ **There are 72 apple trees in the orchard arranged in 9 equal rows. How many apple trees are there in each row? Be sure to show your work.**

A 7

B 8

C 9

D 10

Common Core Standard 6.RP.A.2 – Ratios & Proportional Relationships

☐ **Mr. Baker creates 35 math test problems in 5 hours for the upcoming math pop quiz. How many questions does Mr. Baker create in 3 hours? Be sure to show your work.**

A   21

B   24

C   27

D   30

Common Core Standard 6.RP.A.2 – Ratios & Proportional Relationships

☐ **Fill in the missing number in the statement below. Be sure to show your work.**

224 passengers in 7 buses = _____ passengers per bus

A   30

B   32

C   34

D   36

Common Core Standard 6.RP.A.2 – Ratios & Proportional Relationships

☐ **Nicholas decided to go on a diet. He lost 3 pounds every week. If he keeps losing weight at the same rate, how many weeks does he need to lose 18 pounds? Be sure to show your work.**

A   21

B   15

C   9

D   6

Common Core Standard 6.RP.A.2 – Ratios & Proportional Relationships

☐ **Madison arranged 28 dolls in 4 boxes, so that all boxes contain equal number of dolls. How many dolls are in each box? Be sure to show your work.**

A   4

B   7

C   24

D   32

Common Core Standard 6.RP.A.2 – Ratios & Proportional Relationships

☐ **Fill in the missing number in the statement below. Be sure to show your work.**

6 bottles per pack = 24 bottles in ____ packs

A   30

B   18

C   6

D   4

Common Core Standard 6.RP.A.2 – Ratios & Proportional Relationships

☐ **There are 90,000 inhabitants within 15 square miles. How many inhabitants live in 9 square miles? Be sure to show your work.**

A   85,000

B   76,000

C   54,000

D   24,000

Common Core Standard 6.RP.A.2 – Ratios & Proportional Relationships

☐ **In the local newspaper it was reported that scientists found 8 deer in 12 square miles. How many deer do they expect to find in 51 square miles? Be sure to show your work.**

A   20

B   31

C   34

D   39

Common Core Standard 6.RP.A.2 – Ratios & Proportional Relationships

☐ **Fill in the missing number in the statement below. Be sure to show your work.**

_____ words per page = 384 words on 4 pages

A   98

B   96

C   94

D   92

Common Core Standard 6.RP.A.2 – Ratios & Proportional Relationships

☐ **In Easton Middle School out of every 5 students in the school, 2 are girls. There are 355 students in the school. What is the total number of girls in Easton Middle School? Be sure to show your work.**

A   71

B   142

C   213

D   284

Common Core Standard 6.RP.A.2 – Ratios & Proportional Relationships

☐ An automotible factory produced 300 cars in 6 days. If the factory keeps producing cars at the same rate, how many days will the factory need to produce 400 cars? Be sure to show your work.

A   7

B   8

C   9

D   10

Common Core Standard 6.RP.A.2 – Ratios & Proportional Relationships

☐ Fill in the missing number in the statement below. Be sure to show your work.

28 miles per hour = 140 miles in _____ hours

A   7

B   6

C   5

D   4

Common Core Standard 6.RP.A.2 – Ratios & Proportional Relationships

☐ Out of every 8 students at Praston Junior High, 6 students study Spanish. What is the number of students who study Spanish, if the total number of students is 320? Be sure to show your work.

A   80

B   120

C   160

D   240

Common Core Standard 6.RP.A.2 – Ratios & Proportional Relationships

☐ At OvenReady Bakery, the bakery bakes 480 breads in 16 hours. If the bakery keeps baking bread at the same rate, how many breads will it bake in 12 hours? Be sure to show your work.

A   440

B   400

C   360

D   320

Common Core Standard 6.RP.A.2 – Ratios & Proportional Relationships

☐ Fill in the missing number in the statement below. Be sure to show your work.

_____ cherries per bowl = 176 cherries in 8 bowls

A   12

B   15

C   19

D   22

Common Core Standard 6.RP.A.2 – Ratios & Proportional Relationships

☐ Out of 9 animals at the local zoo, 2 are birds. How many birds are at the zoo, if the total number of animals is 81? Be sure to show your work.

A   9

B   18

C   27

D   36

Common Core Standard 6.RP.A.3.A – Ratios & Proportional Relationships

The ratio of boys to girls in Stanton Middle School is 2 to 3. Which of the following ratios is equivalent to the ratio of boys to girls? Be sure to show your work.

A   3 boys to 2 girls

B   4 boys to 3 girls

C   2 boys to 6 girls

D   4 boys to 6 girls

Common Core Standard 6.RP.A.3.A – Ratios & Proportional Relationships

The values in the table below are proportional. Fill in the missing number and be sure to show your work.

A   14

B   15

C   16

D   18

Hours	Miles
2	6
4	12
5	
7	21

Common Core Standard 6.RP.A.3.A – Ratios & Proportional Relationships

Which two fruits in the coordinate plane below have equal ratios of coordinates? Be sure to show your work.

A   Apple and Strawberry

B   Apple and Pear

C   Cherry and Pear

D   Strawberry and Cherry

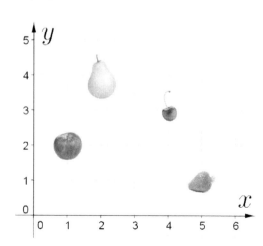

Common Core Standard 6.RP.A.3.A – Ratios & Proportional Relationships

☐ For every six blue cars there are four red cars in the parking lot. Which of the following ratios is equivalent to the ratio of blue cars to red cars? Be sure to show your work.

A   3:2

B   2:3

C   3:4

D   4:3

Common Core Standard 6.RP.A.3.A – Ratios & Proportional Relationships

☐ The values in the table below are proportional. Fill in the missing number and be sure to show your work.

A   12

B   14

C   16

D   18

Bottles	Packs
8	2
	4
20	5
24	6

Common Core Standard 6.RP.A.3.A – Ratios & Proportional Relationships

☐ What is the ratio of coordinates of points which lie on the line in the coordinate plane below? Be sure to show your work.

A   1:3

B   3:2

C   2:1

D   2:3

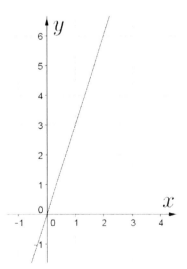

Common Core Standard 6.RP.A.3.A – Ratios & Proportional Relationships

☐ A local thrift store sold 15 shirts in 3 hours. Which of the following ratios is equivalent to the ratio of hours to shirts sold? Be sure to show your work.

A   5:1

B   1:5

C   5:3

D   1:3

Common Core Standard 6.RP.A.3.A – Ratios & Proportional Relationships

☐ The values in the table below are proportional. Fill in the missing number and be sure to show your work.

A   3

B   4

C   5

D   6

Candies	Bags
30	2
60	
105	7
135	9

Common Core Standard 6.RP.A.3.A – Ratios & Proportional Relationships

☐ Which fruit in the coordinate plane below has the greatest ratio of coordinate x to coordinate y? Be sure to show your work.

A   Apple

B   Pear

C   Cherry

D   Strawberry

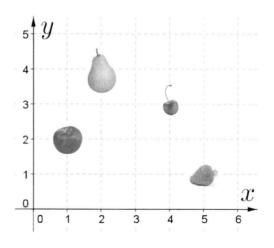

Common Core Standard 6.RP.A.3.A – Ratios & Proportional Relationships

☐ For every six horses there are eight cows on the farm. Which of the following ratios is equivalent to the ratio of cows to horses? Be sure to show your work.

A   3:8

B   4:6

C   3:4

D   4:3

Common Core Standard 6.RP.A.3.A – Ratios & Proportional Relationships

☐ The values in the table below are proportional. Fill in the missing number and be sure to show your work.

A   2

B   4

C   5

D   7

Clovers	Leaves
3	9
	15
6	18
8	24

Common Core Standard 6.RP.A.3.A – Ratios & Proportional Relationships

☐ What is the ratio of coordinates of dog and cat in the coordinate plane below? Be sure to show your work.

A   2:1

B   4:1

C   1:4

D   2:3

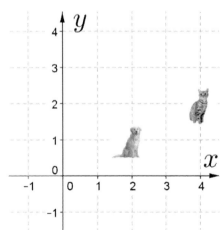

Common Core Standard 6.RP.A.3.A – Ratios & Proportional Relationships

☐   Joshua had 2 incorrect answers for every 8 correct answers on his math test. Which of the following ratios is equivalent to the ratio of incorrect to correct answers? Be sure to show your work.

A   1:4

B   4:1

C   1:5

D   5:1

Common Core Standard 6.RP.A.3.A – Ratios & Proportional Relationships

☐   The values in the table below are proportional. Fill in the missing number and be sure to show your work.

A   12

B   14

C   16

D   18

Cars	Wheels
2	8
4	
6	24
8	32

Common Core Standard 6.RP.A.3.A – Ratios & Proportional Relationships

☐   What is the ratio of x coordinate to y coordinate of the ball in the coordinate plane below? Be sure to show your work.

A   2:1

B   1:2

C   2:3

D   1:3

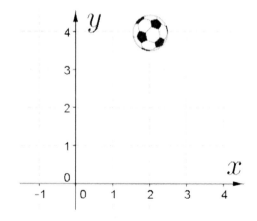

Name_____

Common Core Standard 6.RP.A.3.A – Ratios & Proportional Relationships

☐ There are 6 women for every 4 men in Sam's father's company. Which of the following ratios is equivalent to the ratio of men to women? Be sure to show your work.

A   3:5

B   2:5

C   3:2

D   2:3

Common Core Standard 6.RP.A.3.A – Ratios & Proportional Relationships

☐ The values in the table below are proportional. Fill in the missing number and be sure to show your work.

A   7

B   6

C   5

D   4

Legs	Dogs
8	2
20	
32	8
40	10

Common Core Standard 6.RP.A.3.A – Ratios & Proportional Relationships

☐ What is the ratio of coordinates of points which lie on the line in the coordinate plane below? Be sure to show your work.

A   2:1

B   3:1

C   2:3

D   3:4

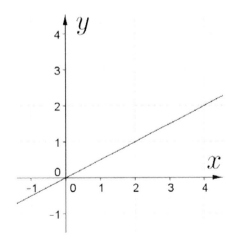

Common Core Standard 6.RP.A.3.A – Ratios & Proportional Relationships

☐ The ratio of baseball pitchers to catchers in Mike's baseball league is 4 to 1. Which of the following is equivalent to this ratio? Be sure to show your work.

A   32 pitchers to 16 catchers

B   32 pitchers to 8 catchers

C   32 pitchers to 16 catchers

D   32 pitchers to 4 catchers

Common Core Standard 6.RP.A.3.A – Ratios & Proportional Relationships

☐ The values in the table below are proportional. Fill in the missing number and be sure to show your work.

A $12

B $15

C $18

D $21

Breads	Price
4	$10
6	
8	$20
10	$25

Common Core Standard 6.RP.A.3.A – Ratios & Proportional Relationships

☐ Which object in the coordinate plane below has the ratio of coordinates 3 to 1? Be sure to show your work.

A   Chair

B   Hat

C   Bulb

D   Balloon

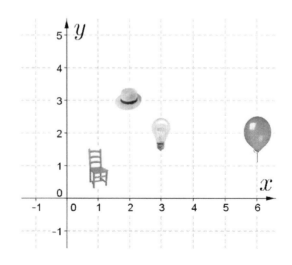

Common Core Standard 6.RP.A.3.A – Ratios & Proportional Relationships

☐ On the Longview professional basketball team there are 2 Europeans for every 8 Americans. Which of the following is equivalent to this ratio? Be sure to show your work.

A   1 European to 5 Americans

B   4 Americans to 5 Europeans

C   1 European to 4 Americans

D   1 American to 5 Europeans

Common Core Standard 6.RP.A.3.A – Ratios & Proportional Relationships

☐ The values in the table below are proportional. Fill in the missing number and be sure to show your work.

A   3

B   4

C   5

D   6

Bottles	Weight
2	3 liters
	9 liters
8	12 liters
10	15 liters

Common Core Standard 6.RP.A.3.A – Ratios & Proportional Relationships

☐ Which object in the coordinate plane below has the lowest ratio of coordinate y to coordinate x? Be sure to show your work.

A   Chair

B   Hat

C   Bulb

D   Balloon

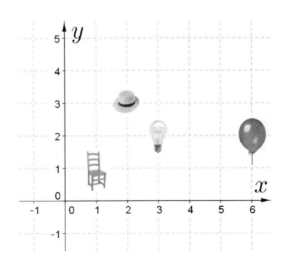

Common Core Standard 6.RP.A.3.B – Ratios & Proportional Relationships

☐ Benjamin's father is a writer working on his new book. He wrote 33 pages of his new book in 6 days. At this rate, how many pages will Benjamin's father write in 8 days? Be sure to show your work.

A   40

B   42

C   44

D   46

Common Core Standard 6.RP.A.3.B – Ratios & Proportional Relationships

☐ Sonia wants to buy 0.4 kg of honey. The price of honey is $8/kg. How much will Sonia pay for 0.4 kg of honey? Be sure to show your work.

A $3.00

B $3.20

C $3.40

D $3.60

Common Core Standard 6.RP.A.3.B – Ratios & Proportional Relationships

☐ David rode a bicycle at a constant speed in a local bike race. He rode 36 miles in 3 hours. What was the speed David rode his bicycle in the race? Be sure to show your work.

A   18 mi/h

B   16 mi/h

C   14 mi/h

D   12 mi/h

Common Core Standard 6.RP.A.3.B – Ratios & Proportional Relationships

☐ **Miles of Smiles Toy Factory creates 168 toys in 12 hours. At this rate, how many toys does Miles of Smiles Toy Factory create in 5 hours? Be sure to show your work.**

A   70

B   74

C   80

D   84

Common Core Standard 6.RP.A.3.B – Ratios & Proportional Relationships

☐ **Lillie bought 12 lb of apples for $16. How many pounds of apples can Lily buy for $20? Be sure to show your work.**

A   15 lb

B   16 lb

C   17 lb

D   18 lb

Common Core Standard 6.RP.A.3.B – Ratios & Proportional Relationships

☐ **The speed of the school bus is 60 miles per hour. How many miles will the bus go in 2 hours and 15 minutes? Be sure to show your work.**

A   125

B   130

C   135

D   140

Common Core Standard 6.RP.A.3.B – Ratios & Proportional Relationships

☐ Carter read 48 pages in 6 minutes. How many pages, at that rate, will Carter read in 10 minutes? Be sure to show your work.

A   60

B   70

C   80

D   90

Common Core Standard 6.RP.A.3.B – Ratios & Proportional Relationships

☐ Julieta sells hand-crocheted baby booties. The price of 6 booties is $111. What is the price of 4 booties? Be sure to show your work.

A $68

B $70

C $72

D $74

Common Core Standard 6.RP.A.3.B – Ratios & Proportional Relationships

☐ What is the average speed of plane that passes 2,500 miles in 4 hours? Be sure to show your work.

A   600 mi/h

B   625 mi/h

C   650 mi/h

D   675 mi/h

Common Core Standard 6.RP.A.3.B – Ratios & Proportional Relationships

☐ **It is expected 2 sunny days per week in February. What is the expected number of sunny days in February? Be sure to show your work.**

A   2

B   4

C   6

D   8

Common Core Standard 6.RP.A.3.B – Ratios & Proportional Relationships

☐ **Samantha paid $56 for 12 pairs of socks. What is the price of 9 pairs of socks? Be sure to show your work.**

A $42

B $44

C $46

D $48

Common Core Standard 6.RP.A.3.B – Ratios & Proportional Relationships

☐ **What must be the speed of a car so that distance of 140 miles is passed in 1 hour and 45 minutes? Be sure to show your work.**

A   65 mi/h

B   70 mi/h

C   75 mi/h

D   80 mi/h

Common Core Standard 6.RP.A.3.B – Ratios & Proportional Relationships

☐ **12 bottles contain 18 liters of soda. How many bottles contain 12 liters of soda? Be sure to show your work.**

A   6

B   8

C   10

D   18

Common Core Standard 6.RP.A.3.B – Ratios & Proportional Relationships

☐ **Michael sells tickets to a football game. He sold 321 tickets in 3 hours. How many tickets, at that rate, will he sell in 5 hours? Be sure to show your work.**

A   535

B   540

C   545

D   550

Common Core Standard 6.RP.A.3.B – Ratios & Proportional Relationships

☐ **Zoe travelled by bus. She travelled first 2 hours at a constant speed of 60 mi/h, and next 3 hours at a constant speed of 70 mi/h. What is the distance that Zoe travelled in 5 hours? Be sure to show your work.**

A   300 miles

B   315 miles

C   330 miles

D   350 miles

Name_____

Common Core Standard 6.RP.A.3.B – Ratios & Proportional Relationships

☐ There are 48 marbles in 8 bags. How many marbles are there in 5 bags? Be sure to show your work.

A   20

B   25

C   30

D   35

Common Core Standard 6.RP.A.3.B – Ratios & Proportional Relationships

☐ Lydia bought 3 pens for $4.20 and 2 erasers for $1.20. Maya bought a pen and an eraser. How much did Maya pay? Be sure to show your work.

A $1.00

B $1.50

C $2.00

D $2.50

Common Core Standard 6.RP.A.3.B – Ratios & Proportional Relationships

☐ Peter travelled by train and passed 150 miles in 3 hours. Then the train increased its speed by 10 mi/h. How long did Peter travel next 120 miles? Be sure to show your work.

A   1 hour and 45 minutes

B   2 hours

C   2 hours and 15 minutes

D   2 hours and 30 minutes

Common Core Standard 6.RP.A.3.B – Ratios & Proportional Relationships

☐ The students are going on a trip. There are 150 students in 6 buses. How many buses are needed for 250 students? Be sure to show your work.

A   7

B   8

C   9

D   10

Common Core Standard 6.RP.A.3.B – Ratios & Proportional Relationships

☐ The price of apples is $4/kg and the price of oranges is $6/kg. Maria bought 2.5 kg of apples and 1.5 kg of oranges. How much did Maria pay? Be sure to show your work.

A $16

B $19

C $22

D $24

Common Core Standard 6.RP.A.3.B – Ratios & Proportional Relationships

☐ A car is travelling at the constant speed of 45 mi/h. How many miles will the car pass in 2 hours and 20 minutes? Be sure to show your work.

A   95 miles

B   100 miles

C   105 miles

D   110 miles

Name_____

Common Core Standard 6.RP.A.3.B – Ratios & Proportional Relationships

☐ Molly makes 3 cakes in 7 hours. How many hours does she need to make 9 cakes? Be sure to show your work.

A   10

B   12

C   16

D   21

Common Core Standard 6.RP.A.3.B – Ratios & Proportional Relationships

☐ The price for 5 balls is $35. The price of sneakers is $25 per pair. How much would Dominic pay for 3 balls and 2 pairs of sneakers? Be sure to show your work.

A $71

B $91

C $125

D $155

Common Core Standard 6.RP.A.3.B – Ratios & Proportional Relationships

☐ Adam travelled 4 hours at the speed of 75 mi/h and 3 hours at the speed of 40 mi/h. What is the average speed of his journey? Be sure to show your work.

A   57.5 mi/h

B   60 mi/h

C   62.5 mi/h

D   65 mi/h

Common Core Standard 6.RP.A.3.C – Ratios & Proportional Relationships

☐ **There are 540 people watching the basketball game. 25% of them are supporters of the guest team. How many supporters of the guest team are watching a basketball game? Be sure to show your work.**

A   25

B   90

C   135

D   250

Common Core Standard 6.RP.A.3.C – Ratios & Proportional Relationships

☐ **Fill in the missing number to find the correct answer below.**

8% of 350 = _____

A   8

B   16

C   28

D   36

Common Core Standard 6.RP.A.3.C – Ratios & Proportional Relationships

☐ **There are 144 girls in the school, which is 18% of all the students. How many students are there in the school? Be sure to show your work.**

A   900

B   800

C   700

D   600

Name_____

Common Core Standard 6.RP.A.3.C – Ratios & Proportional Relationships

☐ Grace bought a pair of pants on sale for $24, which is 60% off of the original price. What was the original price of the pants? Be sure to show your work.

A $24

B $36

C $48

D $60

Common Core Standard 6.RP.A.3.C – Ratios & Proportional Relationships

☐ Fill in the missing number to find the correct answer below.

$$\text{\_\_\_\_}\% \text{ of } 1200 = 48$$

A 2

B 4

C 6

D 8

Common Core Standard 6.RP.A.3.C – Ratios & Proportional Relationships

☐ 120 third graders voted for the most popular teacher. 6 of them voted for a math teacher. What percentage of students voted for a math teacher? Be sure to show your work.

A 2%

B 5%

C 6%

D 12%

Name_____

Common Core Standard 6.RP.A.3.C – Ratios & Proportional Relationships

☐ A box of 600 bulbs contains 3% of improper bulbs. How many improper bulbs are there in a box? Be sure to show your work.

A 3

B 9

C 18

D 24

Common Core Standard 6.RP.A.3.C – Ratios & Proportional Relationships

☐ Fill in the missing number to find the correct answer below.

70% of ____ = 98

A 125

B 130

C 135

D 140

Common Core Standard 6.RP.A.3.C – Ratios & Proportional Relationships

☐ The first part of the math test lasts 20 minutes, which is 40% of the time provided for the test. How long does the test last? Be sure to show your work.

A 45 minutes

B 50 minutes

C 55 minutes

D 60 minutes

Common Core Standard 6.RP.A.3.C – Ratios & Proportional Relationships

☐ The price of the shirt on sale is 80% of the original price. If the original price was $35, what is the price of the shirt on sale? Be sure to show your work.

A $32

B $30

C $28

D $26

Common Core Standard 6.RP.A.3.C – Ratios & Proportional Relationships

☐ Fill in the missing number to find the correct answer below.

15% of 240 = ____

A   15

B   18

C   30

D   36

Common Core Standard 6.RP.A.3.C – Ratios & Proportional Relationships

☐ Peter' bill at the café was $60. He left a 15% tip. What was the amount of the tip? Be sure to show your work.

A $7

B $8

C $9

D $10

Common Core Standard 6.RP.A.3.C – Ratios & Proportional Relationships

☐ There are 48 cars on the parking lot, and 36 cars are 5 or less years old. What is the percentage of cars older than 5 years on the parking lot? Be sure to show your work.

A   25%

B   45%

C   65%

D   75%

Common Core Standard 6.RP.A.3.C – Ratios & Proportional Relationships

☐ Fill in the missing number to find the correct answer below.

____% of 150 = 9

A   3

B   6

C   9

D   12

Common Core Standard 6.RP.A.3.C – Ratios & Proportional Relationships

☐ Arin read 24 pages, which is 8% of the book. How many pages are left for Arin to finish the book? Be sure to show your work.

A   300

B   276

C   220

D   192

Name_____

Common Core Standard 6.RP.A.3.C – Ratios & Proportional Relationships

☐ There are 2 green, 6 red, and 8 blue marbles in the bag. What is the percentage of green marbles in the bag? Be sure to show your work.

A   2%

B   4.5%

C   8

D   12.5%

Common Core Standard 6.RP.A.3.C – Ratios & Proportional Relationships

☐ Fill in the missing number to find the correct answer below.

$$46\% \text{ of } \underline{\qquad} = 161$$

A   350

B   355

C   360

D   365

Common Core Standard 6.RP.A.3.C – Ratios & Proportional Relationships

☐ Michael scored 22 points in the basketball game, which is 25% of all the points that his team scored in a game. How many points did Michael's team scored? Be sure to show your work.

A   99

B   88

C   77

D   66

Common Core Standard 6.RP.A.3.C – Ratios & Proportional Relationships

☐ **The international science forum consists of Americans and Asians. There are 20 Americans, which is 16% of all scientists. How many Asians are there in the science forum? Be sure to show your work.**

A   125

B   105

C   84

D   36

Common Core Standard 6.RP.A.3.C – Ratios & Proportional Relationships

☐ **Fill in the missing number to find the correct answer below.**

34% of 150 = _____

A   17

B   34

C   51

D   68

Common Core Standard 6.RP.A.3.C – Ratios & Proportional Relationships

☐ **Marry fosters 20 pets: 25% are dogs, 20% are cats, and the rest are parots. How many parots does Marry foster? Be sure to show your work.**

A   4

B   5

C   9

D   11

Name_____

Common Core Standard 6.RP.A.3.C – Ratios & Proportional Relationships

☐ 3/4 of the surface of Earth is covered with water. What percentage of Earth's surface is covered with land? Be sure to show your work.

A   25%

B   50%

C   75%

D   100%

Common Core Standard 6.RP.A.3.C – Ratios & Proportional Relationships

☐ Fill in the missing number to find the correct answer below.

____% of 360 = 54

A   12

B   13

C   14

D   15

Common Core Standard 6.RP.A.3.C – Ratios & Proportional Relationships

☐ Peter, Michael, and John ate a cake. John ate 2/5 of a cake. What percentage of cake did Michael and John eat? Be sure to show your work.

A   20%

B   40%

C   60%

D   80%

Common Core Standard 6.RP.A.3.D – Ratios & Proportional Relationships

☐ **Madison bought 2 lbs of sugar for $3.20. What is the price of sugar per oz? Be sure to show your work.**

A $0.10

B $0.15

C $0.20

D $0.25

Common Core Standard 6.RP.A.3.D – Ratios & Proportional Relationships

☐ **Fill in the missing number to find the correct answer below.**

2.3 km = _____ m

A   23

B   230

C   2,300

D   23,000

Common Core Standard 6.RP.A.3.D – Ratios & Proportional Relationships

☐ **Benjamin poured 1 gallon and 3 quarts of water into the pot. How many more quarts does he need to pour to have 2 gallons of water in the pot? Be sure to show your work.**

A   1

B   2

C   3

D   4

Name_____

Common Core Standard 6.RP.A.3.D – Ratios & Proportional Relationships

☐ **Abigail weighed her doll. The weight of her doll was 250 g. How much did Abigail's doll weigh in kilograms? Be sure to show your work.**

A   0.025 kg

B   0.25 kg

C   2.5 kg

D   25 kg

Common Core Standard 6.RP.A.3.D – Ratios & Proportional Relationships

☐ **Fill in the missing number to find the correct answer below.**

_____ yd = 12 ft

A   3

B   4

C   24

D   36

Common Core Standard 6.RP.A.3.D – Ratios & Proportional Relationships

☐ **Tyler drank 400 mL of juice. How many liters of juice did Tyler drink? Be sure to show your work.**

A   4,000 L

B   40 L

C   4 L

D   0.4 L

Common Core Standard 6.RP.A.3.D – Ratios & Proportional Relationships

☐ **Liana's car weighs a ton. How many pounds does Liana's car weigh? Be sure to show your work.**

A   250 lb

B   500 lb

C   1,000 lb

D   2,000 lb

Common Core Standard 6.RP.A.3.D – Ratios & Proportional Relationships

☐ **Fill in the missing number to find the correct answer below.**

150 cm = _____ m

A   0.015

B   0.15

C   1.5

D   15

Common Core Standard 6.RP.A.3.D – Ratios & Proportional Relationships

☐ **Joey bought 2 quarts of tea for $12. What is the price of tea per cup? Be sure to show your work.**

A $0.75

B $1.5

C $3

D $6

Name_____

Common Core Standard 6.RP.A.3.D – Ratios & Proportional Relationships

☐ The average weight of an adult male elephant is 6 tons. How many kilograms does an adult male elephant weigh? Be sure to show your work.

A   60 kg

B   600 kg

C   6,000 kg

D   60,000 kg

Common Core Standard 6.RP.A.3.D – Ratios & Proportional Relationships

☐ Fill in the missing number to find the correct answer below.

_____ ft = 24 in

A   2

B   3

C   48

D   72

Common Core Standard 6.RP.A.3.D – Ratios & Proportional Relationships

☐ A bottle contains 2 liters of root beer. How many milliliters of root beer does a bottle contain? Be sure to show your work.

A   500 mL

B   1,000 mL

C   2,000 mL

D   4,000 mL

Name_____

Common Core Standard 6.RP.A.3.D – Ratios & Proportional Relationships

☐ A dog weighs 5 lb 8 oz, and a cat weighs 4 lb 10 oz. How much do they weigh together? Be sure to show your work.

A   10 lb 2 oz

B   9 lb 10 oz

C   9 lb 8 oz

D   9 lb 2 oz

Common Core Standard 6.RP.A.3.D – Ratios & Proportional Relationships

☐ Calculate the problem below to find the correct answer.

2 km 600 m + 3 km 500 m = _____ m

A   6.1

B   61

C   610

D   6,100

Common Core Standard 6.RP.A.3.D – Ratios & Proportional Relationships

☐ Jordan is making juice punch. He poured 12 fl oz of apple juice into the glass, 18 fl oz of orange juice, and 2 fl oz of cherry mix. What is the volume of the juice punch in cups? Be sure to show your work.

A   1

B   2

C   3

D   4

Name_____

Common Core Standard 6.RP.A.3.D – Ratios & Proportional Relationships

☐ The average weight of a cow is 300 kg, and the average weight of a horse is 600 kg. How many tons do cow and horse weigh together? Be sure to show your work.

A   0.9 tons

B   1 tons

C   4.5 tons

D   9 tons

Common Core Standard 6.RP.A.3.D – Ratios & Proportional Relationships

☐ Calculate the problem below to find the correct answer.

2 ft 8 in + 5 ft 4 in = _____ ft

A   7

B   8

C   9

D   10

Common Core Standard 6.RP.A.3.D – Ratios & Proportional Relationships

☐ Sarah poured 800 mL of coffee in 4 cups, and 700 mL of coffee in 3 cups. How many liters of coffee did Sarah pour in 7 cups? Be sure to show your work.

A   0.015 L

B   0.15 L

C   1.5 L

D   15 L

Common Core Standard 6.RP.A.3.D – Ratios & Proportional Relationships

A basketball weighs 2 lb 9 oz, and a football weighs 1 lb 12 oz. How many more ounces does a basketball weigh than a football? Be sure to show your work.

A   3 oz

B   9 oz

C   12 oz

D   13 oz

Common Core Standard 6.RP.A.3.D – Ratios & Proportional Relationships

Calculate the problem below to find the correct answer.

$$3 \text{ m } 2 \text{ dm} - 2\text{m } 8 \text{ dm} = \underline{\hspace{2cm}} \text{ dm}$$

A   2

B   4

C   6

D   8

Common Core Standard 6.RP.A.3.D – Ratios & Proportional Relationships

There was a quart of mineral water in a jug. Peter drank 2 cups. How many pints of mineral water are left in a jug? Be sure to show your work.

A   1 pt

B   2 pt

C   3 pt

D   4 pt

Name_____

Common Core Standard 6.RP.A.3.D – Ratios & Proportional Relationships

☐ Anna bought 3.5 kg of pears and 2.8 kg of peaches. How many more grams of pears did Anna buy than peaches? Be sure to show your work.

A   0.7 gm

B   7 gm

C   70 gm

D   700 gm

Common Core Standard 6.RP.A.3.D – Ratios & Proportional Relationships

☐ Fill in the missing number to find the correct anwer below.

5 yd 1 ft – 4 yd 2 ft = ____ ft

A   1

B   2

C   3

D   4

Common Core Standard 6.RP.A.3.D – Ratios & Proportional Relationships

☐ There was a liter of water in a bottle. 20 mL evaporated. How many milliliters of water are left in a bottle? Be sure to show your work.

A   80 mL

B   980 mL

C   9,980 mL

D   99,980 mL

Name_____

Common Core Standard 6.NS.A.1 – The Number System

☐ **Elizabeth studied a history lesson for 2 hours. She finished each section in half an hour. How many sections did she complete? Be sure to show your work.**

A   1

B   2

C   3

D   4

Common Core Standard 6.NS.A.1 – The Number System

☐ **The area of rectangular piece of wood is 3/8 square yard. How long is the rectangular piece of wood, if its width is 3/4 yard. Be sure to show your work.**

A   1/2 yard

B   1/3 yard

C   2/3 yard

D   1/4 yard

Common Core Standard 6.NS.A.1 – The Number System

☐ **3 friends shared equally 2/3 kg of ice cream. How much ice cream did each of them get? Be sure to show your work.**

A   2 kg

B   3 kg

C   2/9 kg

D   1/3 kg

Common Core Standard 6.NS.A.1 – The Number System

☐ **A glass contains 1/5 liter of water. How many glasses of water are needed to fill a bottle of 1 liter? Be sure to show your work.**

A   1

B   2

C   5

D   10

Common Core Standard 6.NS.A.1 – The Number System

☐ **How many ounces of sugar are in a bag of 3/4 lb? (1 oz = 1/16 lb)   Be sure to show your work.**

A   3 oz

B   4 oz

C   8 oz

D   12 oz

Common Core Standard 6.NS.A.1 – The Number System

☐ **Kaleb divided equally 6/7 lb of strawberries in 3 plates. How much strawberries did Kaleb put in each plate? Be sure to show your work.**

A   2/7 lb

B   3/7 lb

C   4/7 lb

D   5/7 lb

Name_____

Common Core Standard 6.NS.A.1 – The Number System

☐ Ava has 4 kg of honey. She served honey in cups of 2/3 kg. How many cups did she serve?   Be sure to show your work.

A   3

B   4

C   6

D   8

Common Core Standard 6.NS.A.1 – The Number System

☐ The stick is 2/3 yd long. How many feet long is the stick? (1 ft = 1/3 yd) Be sure to show your work.

A   2 ft

B   3 ft

C   5 ft

D   6 ft

Common Core Standard 6.NS.A.1 – The Number System

☐ Anahit poured 1/2 liter of juice in 4 glasses. What is the volume of each glass? Be sure to show your work.

A   2 liters

B   1 liters

C   1/4 liters

D   1/8 liters

Common Core Standard 6.NS.A.1 – The Number System

☐ For Halloween, David packed 6 lb of candy into bags of 1/3 lb each. How many bags of candy did David pack? Be sure to show your work.

A   3

B   6

C   9

D   18

Common Core Standard 6.NS.A.1 – The Number System

☐ The area of rectangular tile is 1/2 square feet. How wide is a rectangular tile, if its length is 3/4 ft? Be sure to show your work.

A   1/3 ft

B   2/3 ft

C   1/4 ft

D   2/5 ft

Common Core Standard 6.NS.A.1 – The Number System

☐ A board is 3 m long. It is cut in pieces of 3/4 m. How many pieces of board are cut? Be sure to show your work.

A   3

B   4

C   6

D   8

Name_____

Common Core Standard 6.NS.A.1 – The Number System

□   Hannah served 2 liters of tea in cups of 1/4 l each. How many cups of tea did Hannah serve? Be sure to show your work.

    A   2

    B   4

    C   8

    D   16

Common Core Standard 6.NS.A.1 – The Number System

□   The area of a painting is 3/8 square yard. How wide is the painting, if its length is 3/5 yards? Be sure to show your work.

    A   2/5 yd

    B   5/8 yd

    C   2/3 yd

    D   2/8 yd

Common Core Standard 6.NS.A.1 – The Number System

□   14 mine workers dug out 7/2 tons of coal, equally. How much coal did each of them dig out? Be sure to show your work.

    A   1/2 t

    B   1/3 t

    C   1/4 t

    D   1/5 t

Name_____

Common Core Standard 6.NS.A.1 – The Number System

☐ A pack contains 9 liters of soda in bottles of 3/2 l each. How many bottles are there in the pack? Be sure to show your work.

A   4

B   6

C   9

D   12

Common Core Standard 6.NS.A.1 – The Number System

☐ At a local jewelry store one golden chain weighs 1/12 lb. How many golden chains can be made of 1/4 lb of gold? Be sure to show your work.

A   3

B   4

C   6

D   9

Common Core Standard 6.NS.A.1 – The Number System

☐ 5 pond fish equally consumed 5/8 kg of fish food. How much fish food did each of them get? Be sure to show your work.

A   1/2 kg

B   1/4 kg

C   1/5 kg

D   1/8 kg

Common Core Standard 6.NS.A.1 – The Number System

☐ **Marry served 9 lb of salad in bowls of 3/4 lb each. How many bowls did she serve? Be sure to show your work.**

A   3

B   4

C   9

D   12

Common Core Standard 6.NS.A.1 – The Number System

☐ **A worm is 2/3 ft long. How many inches long is the worm? (1 in = 1/12 ft) Be sure to show your work.**

A   2 in

B   3 in

C   8 in

D   12 in

Common Core Standard 6.NS.A.1 – The Number System

☐ **4 jewelers shared equally 3/4 kg of silver. How much silver did each of them get? Be sure to show your work.**

A   1/3 kg

B   1/4 kg

C   3/8 kg

D   3/16 kg

Common Core Standard 6.NS.A.1 – The Number System

☐ How many 1/3 m long stripes can be made of 4 m of material? Be sure to show your work.

A   3

B   4

C   7

D   12

Common Core Standard 6.NS.A.1 – The Number System

☐ A motorcycle is 3 m long. How many decimeters long is the motorcycle? (1 dm = 1/10 m) Be sure to show your work.

A   3 dm

B   10 dm

C   30 dm

D   33 dm

Common Core Standard 6.NS.A.1 – The Number System

☐ 6/7 l of milk is poured equally in 3 glasses. How much milk does each glass contain? Be sure to show your work.

A   2/7 liters

B   3/7 liters

C   3/6 liters

D   2/3 liters

Common Core Standard 6.NS.B.2 – The Number System

☐ There are 1,150 students in the school. They attend classrooms with 25 seats. If each classroom has equal amount of students, how many classrooms are there in the school? Be sure to show your work.

A 40

B 42

C 44

D 46

Common Core Standard 6.NS.B.2 – The Number System

☐ The area of the tennis court is 2,808 square feet. How wide is the tennis court, if its length is 78 feet? Be sure to show your work.

A 36 ft

B 40 ft

C 44 ft

D 48 ft

Common Core Standard 6.NS.B.2 – The Number System

☐ At a charity event, Olivia sold 45 pairs of shoes and raised $1,710. What was the price of one pair of shoes? Be sure to show your work.

A $28

B $38

C $48

D $58

Common Core Standard 6.NS.B.2 – The Number System

☐   A box of cupcakes weighs 125 g. Markus bought 5 kg of cupcakes. How many boxes of cupcakes did Markus buy? Be sure to show your work.

   A   25

   B   30

   C   35

   D   40

Common Core Standard 6.NS.B.2 – The Number System

☐   540 students are going on a trip. They are travelling in buses of 45 seats each. How many buses will be needed? Be sure to show your work.

   A   11

   B   12

   C   13

   D   14

Common Core Standard 6.NS.B.2 – The Number System

☐   Football team has 11 players. How many football teams can be formed of 352 players? Be sure to show your work.

   A   30

   B   31

   C   32

   D   33

Common Core Standard 6.NS.B.2 – The Number System

☐ Sophia arranged 672 flowers in bouquets. Each bouquet consists of a dozen flowers. How many bouquets did Sophia make? Be sure to show your work.

A 53

B 54

C 55

D 56

Common Core Standard 6.NS.B.2 – The Number System

☐ 1856 fish are divided equally in store aquariums. If each aquarium has 32 fish, how many aquariums are there in the store? Be sure to show your work.

A 49

B 52

C 55

D 58

Common Core Standard 6.NS.B.2 – The Number System

☐ The number of soldiers in a troop is 150. How many troops can be formed of 4,800 soldiers? Be sure to show your work.

A 30

B 32

C 34

D 36

Name_____

Common Core Standard 6.NS.B.2 – The Number System

☐ A truck can transport 115 boxes. How many trucks will be needed to transport 5,175 boxes? Be sure to show your work.

A   35

B   40

C   45

D   50

Common Core Standard 6.NS.B.2 – The Number System

☐ On an average 9-car train has a seating capacity of 873 passengers. What is a seating capacity per car? Be sure to show your work.

A   96

B   97

C   98

D   99

Common Core Standard 6.NS.B.2 – The Number System

☐ A rugby team has 22 players: 15 on the field and 7 on the banch. How many rugby teams can be formed of 2,310 players? Be sure to show your work.

A   105

B   154

C   231

D   330

Common Core Standard 6.NS.B.2 – The Number System

☐ The movie theater has 1,352 seats arranged in 52 rows. How many seats are there in each row? Be sure to show your work.

A   13

B   26

C   52

D   104

Common Core Standard 6.NS.B.2 – The Number System

☐ The area of the basketball court is 4,700 square feet. How wide is the basketball court if its length is 94 ft? Be sure to show your work.

A   50 ft

B   55 ft

C   60 ft

D   65 ft

Common Core Standard 6.NS.B.2 – The Number System

☐ A bag of coffee weighs 450 g. Lusine bought 9 kg of coffee for her café. How many packs of coffee did Lusine buy? Be sure to show your work.

A   14

B   16

C   18

D   20

Name_____

Common Core Standard 6.NS.B.2 – The Number System

☐ RTD's new commuter rail vehicle has passenger capacity of 2,784 passengers. If the passenger capacity per car is 232, what is the number of cars? Be sure to show your work.

A   9

B   10

C   11

D   12

Common Core Standard 6.NS.B.2 – The Number System

☐ There are 1,296 soldiers in a barrack. They are sleeping in 54 rooms. How many soldiers are sleeping in each room? Be sure to show your work.

A   22

B   24

C   26

D   28

Common Core Standard 6.NS.B.2 – The Number System

☐ There are 448 pigeons equally divided in 8 cages. How many pigeons are there in each cage? Be sure to show your work.

A   52

B   54

C   56

D   58

Name_____

Common Core Standard 6.NS.B.2 – The Number System

☐ Guests at Herman's birthday party drank 1,920 fl oz of juice. How many gallons of juice did they drink? (1 gal = 128 fl. oz)   Be sure to show your work.

A   15

B   16

C   17

D   18

Common Core Standard 6.NS.B.2 – The Number System

☐ The football field is 1,944 in wide. How many yards is the football field's width? (1 yd = 36 in) Be sure to show your work.

A   50 yd

B   52 yd

C   54 yd

D   56 yd

Common Core Standard 6.NS.B.2 – The Number System

☐ There are 2,108 books in the library. The library is relocating to another location, so the books are being packed in 34 boxes, equally. How many books are in each box? Be sure to show your work.

A   60

B   62

C   64

D   66

Name_____

Common Core Standard 6.NS.B.2 – The Number System

☐ The weight of 16 go-carts is 3,600 kg. How much does one go-cart weigh? Be sure to show your work.

A 215 kg

B 220 kg

C 225 kg

D 230 kg

Common Core Standard 6.NS.B.2 – The Number System

☐ Connor sold 9 kg of popcorn. If he sold popcorn in bags of 125 g each, how many bags did he sell? Be sure to show your work.

A 70

B 72

C 74

D 76

Common Core Standard 6.NS.B.2 – The Number System

☐ The area of the boxing ring is 529 square feet. How wide is the boxing ring if its length is 23 ft? Be sure to show your work.

A 20 ft

B 21 ft

C 22 ft

D 23 ft

Common Core Standard 6.NS.B.3 – The Number System

☐ Kristine bought 3 shirts on sale. The price of each shirt was $8.95. How much did she pay in all, before tax? Be sure to show your work.

A $26.85

B $27.15

C $27.85

D $28.15

Common Core Standard 6.NS.B.3 – The Number System

☐ Fill in the missing number to find the correct answer below.

$$(2.25 \div 5 - 0.15) \times 0.5 = \rule{2cm}{0.4pt}$$

A   0.30

B   0.25

C   0.20

D   0.15

Common Core Standard 6.NS.B.3 – The Number System

☐ Ethan likes to ride his bicycle on the weekends. On Sunday, he crossed 33.6 miles in 4 hours. What was his average speed per hour on Sunday? Be sure to show your work.

A   8.2 mi/h

B   8.4 mi/h

C   8.6 mi/h

D   8.8 mi/h

Common Core Standard 6.NS.B.3 – The Number System

☐ A chocolate bar costs $4.49 and a bubble gum costs $0.78. What is the price of 2 chocolate bars and 5 bubble gums? Be sure to show your work.

A $10.88

B $11.88

C $12.88

D $13.88

Common Core Standard 6.NS.B.3 – The Number System

☐ Which sign makes the sentence true? Be sure to show your work.

$$6.2 \times 0.4 \text{\_\_\_\_\_} 22.8 \div 3$$

A   >

B   =

C   <

D   ≥

Common Core Standard 6.NS.B.3 – The Number System

☐ Cameron cut the stick in 5 equal pieces. If the length of the stick was 1.5 m, what is the length of each piece? Be sure to show your work.

A   0.3 m

B   0.5 m

C   0.6 m

D   0.8 m

Name_____

Common Core Standard 6.NS.B.3 – The Number System

☐ Jamilia hikes 3.2 km every day. How many kilometers does she hike in 5 days? Be sure to show your work.

A   16 km

B   16.25 km

C   16.75 km

D   17 km

Common Core Standard 6.NS.B.3 – The Number System

☐ Fill in the missing number to find the correct answer below.

$$(4.45 - 2.35) \times 0.2 = \underline{\quad}$$

A   0.32

B   0.42

C   0.52

D   0.62

Common Core Standard 6.NS.B.3 – The Number System

☐ The bag of rice weighs 0.25 kg. How much do 6 bags of rice weigh? Be sure to show your work.

A   1.2 kg

B   1.3 kg

C   1.4 kg

D   1.5 kg

Name_____

Common Core Standard 6.NS.B.3 – The Number System

☐ **Eric is 1.85 m tall, and Sarah is 1.68 m tall. How many meters is Eric taller than Sarah? Be sure to show your work.**

    A   0.07 m

    B   0.17 m

    C   0.27 m

    D   0.37 m

Common Core Standard 6.NS.B.3 – The Number System

☐ **Which sign makes the sentence true? Be sure to show your work.**

$$20.6 \div 4 \underline{\hspace{1cm}} 3.05 + 2.1$$

    A   <

    B   =

    C   >

    D   ≤

Common Core Standard 6.NS.B.3 – The Number System

☐ **The distance between two towns is 72 kilometers. What is the distance between these towns in miles? (1 mi = 1.6 km) Be sure to show your work.**

    A   30 miles

    B   35 miles

    C   45 miles

    D   50 miles

Common Core Standard 6.NS.B.3 – The Number System

☐ **Graham sells records. The price of one record is $3.65. Graham sold 7 records. How much money did he earn? Be sure to show your work.**

A $24.05

B $24.55

C $25.05

D $25.55

Common Core Standard 6.NS.B.3 – The Number System

☐ **Fill in the missing number to find the correct answer below.**

$$6.25 \div (1.35 + 1.15) = \underline{\quad}$$

A 2.5

B 2.75

C 3

D 4

Common Core Standard 6.NS.B.3 – The Number System

☐ **The swimming pool is 25 m wide. It is divided in 8 equal lanes. How wide is each lane? Be sure to show your work.**

A 3.125 m

B 3.175 m

C 3.225 m

D 3.275 m

Name_____

Common Core Standard 6.NS.B.3 – The Number System

☐ The length of each tile is 0.3 m. How many tiles is needed to cover the room which is 4.2 m long? Be sure to show your work.

A   8

B   10

C   12

D   14

Common Core Standard 6.NS.B.3 – The Number System

☐ Which sign makes the sentence true? Be sure to show your work.

$$8.81 - 2.9 \underline{\hspace{1cm}} 2.1 \times 3.2$$

A   >

B   <

C   =

D   ≥

Common Core Standard 6.NS.B.3 – The Number System

☐ Thomas earns $7.50 per hour. How much money does he earn in 7 days if he works 8 hours per day? Be sure to show your work.

A $112.50

B $60

C $52.50

D $420

Common Core Standard 6.NS.B.3 – The Number System

☐ The screen of mobile phone is 8.25 cm long and 6.4 cm wide. What is the area of the screen? Be sure to show your work.

A   52.8 cm²

B   54.8 cm²

C   56.8 cm²

D   58.8 cm²

Common Core Standard 6.NS.B.3 – The Number System

☐ Fill in the missing number to find the correct answer below.

$$5.3 + 1.25 \times 2 = \_\_\_\_$$

A   13.1

B   11.25

C   7.8

D   6.55

Common Core Standard 6.NS.B.3 – The Number System

☐ What is the perimeter of the room with 4.25 m length and 3.75 m width? Be sure to show your work.

A   8 m

B   11.75 m

C   12.25 m

D   16 m

Common Core Standard 6.NS.B.3 – The Number System

☐ The height of the house is 4.5 m. What is the height of the house in feet? (1 ft = 0.3 m) Be sure to show your work.

A   13.5 ft

B   14 ft

C   14.5 ft

D   15 ft

Common Core Standard 6.NS.B.3 – The Number System

☐ Which sign makes the sentence true? Be sure to show your work.

$$16.25 - 8.75 \underline{\hspace{1.5cm}} 2.85 + 4.65$$

A   <

B   >

C   =

D   ≤

Common Core Standard 6.NS.B.3 – The Number System

☐ Lira bought 5 lb of oranges for $18.75. What was the price of oranges per pound? Be sure to show your work.

A $3.65

B $3.75

C $3.85

D $3.95

Common Core Standard 6.NS.B.4 – The Number System

☐ The number of bottles of soda in 6 variety-drink 6-packs is identical to the number of bottles of soda in 4 soda-only 6-packs. What is the least possible number of soda bottles in the 6 variety drink 6-packs? Be sure to show your work.

A   6

B   36

C   24

D   12

Common Core Standard 6.NS.B.4 – The Number System

☐ Which of the following is equal to the problem below?

24 + 36

A   12 (2 +3)

B   12 (2 + 36)

C   12 (24 + 3)

D   12 (24 + 36)

Common Core Standard 6.NS.B.4 – The Number System

☐ There are 45 rabbits and 30 squirels at a local park. How many identical groups of rabbits and squirels can be made with no animals left out? Be sure to show your work.

A   10

B   15

C   20

D   25

Common Core Standard 6.NS.B.4 – The Number System

☐ Cherie makes bouquets of roses. Each bouquet has 6 roses. Emily makes bouquets of tulips. Each bouquet has 8 tulips. The total number of roses is equal to the total number of tulips. What is the least possible number of roses? Be sure to show your work.

A 12

B 16

C 24

D 48

Common Core Standard 6.NS.B.4 – The Number System

☐ Which of the following is equal to the problem below?

$$5 (2x - 3)$$

A 10x - 3

B 7x - 3

C 10x - 8

D 10x - 15

Common Core Standard 6.NS.B.4 – The Number System

☐ There are 15 girls and 10 boys in the class. How many identical groups of boys and girls can be made with no students left over? Be sure to show your work.

A 2

B 3

C 5

D 10

Name_____

Common Core Standard 6.NS.B.4 – The Number System

☐   The number of pillows in 3-bed camp rooms is identical to the number of pillows in 4-bed camp rooms. What is the least possible number of pillows in 4-bed camp rooms? Be sure to show your work.

    A   7

    B   12

    C   24

    D   36

Common Core Standard 6.NS.B.4 – The Number System

☐   Which of the following is equal to the problem below?

$$42x - 36$$

    A $6 (7x - 6)$

    B $42 (x - 36)$

    C $36 (42x - 1)$

    D $6 (42x - 36)$

Common Core Standard 6.NS.B.4 – The Number System

☐   There are 35 forks and 28 spoons in the kitchen. How many identical packs of forks and spoons can be made with no forks or spoons left over? Be sure to show your work.

    A   4

    B   5

    C   6

    D   7

Name_____

Common Core Standard 6.NS.B.4 – The Number System

☐   The candy bars are sold in blue and red bags. There are 12 candy bars in each blue bag, and 15 candy bars in each red bag. If the total number of candy bars in both types of bags is equal, what is the least possible number of candy bars in red bags? Be sure to show your work.

    A   60

    B   48

    C   45

    D   27

Common Core Standard 6.NS.B.4 – The Number System

☐   Which of the following is equal to the problem below?

$$3 (8 + 5)$$

    A   11 + 8

    B   11 + 5

    C   24 + 15

    D   24 + 5

Common Core Standard 6.NS.B.4 – The Number System

☐   There are 18 junior players and 12 senior players in the basketball club. What is the greatest number of identical teams of juniors and seniors with no players left over? Be sure to show your work.

    A   2

    B   3

    C   5

    D   6

Common Core Standard 6.NS.B.4 – The Number System

☐ The van has 10 seats and the mini bus has 18 seats. The number of passengers transported by vans and mini buses each day is identical. What is the least number of passengers transported by vans each day? Be sure to show your work.

A   20

B   36

C   90

D   180

Common Core Standard 6.NS.B.4 – The Number System

☐ Which of the following is equal to the problem below?

$$24 - 20x$$

A   20 (24 – x)

B   24 (1 – 20x)

C   4 (6 – 5x)

D   6 (4 – 5x)

Common Core Standard 6.NS.B.4 – The Number System

☐ There are 36 daisies and 48 orchids. What is the greatest number of identical bouquets of daisies and orchids with no flowers left over? Be sure to show your work.

A   6

B   12

C   18

D   24

Common Core Standard 6.NS.B.4 – The Number System

☐ The apple trees in the orchard are arranged in 8 rows, and the pear trees are arranged in 12 rows. The total number of apple trees in the orchard is identical to the total number of pear trees. What is the least possible number of apple trees in the orchard? Be sure to show your work.

A   24

B   48

C   72

D   96

Common Core Standard 6.NS.B.4 – The Number System

☐ Which of the following is equal to the problem below?

48 + 72

A   24 (2 + 3)

B   24 (48 + 3)

C   24 (2 + 72)

D   24 (48 + 72)

Common Core Standard 6.NS.B.4 – The Number System

☐ There are 90 peaches and 75 apricots. What is the greatest number of identical packs of peaches and apricots with no fruit left over? Be sure to show your work.

A   5

B   10

C   15

D   20

Common Core Standard 6.NS.B.4 – The Number System

☐ The cars on the parking lot are arranged in 10 rows, and motorcycles are arranged in 14 rows. The total number of cars on the parking lot is identical to the total number of motorcycles. What is the least number of cars on the parking lot? Be sure to show your work.

A   24

B   35

C   70

D   140

Common Core Standard 6.NS.B.4 – The Number System

☐ Which of the following is equal to the problem below?

$$3 (4x + 9)$$

A   7x + 12

B   12x + 27

C   12x + 9

D   12x + 12

Common Core Standard 6.NS.B.4 – The Number System

☐ There are 80 pots and 96 plates in the store. What is the greatest number of identical packs of dishes with no pots or plates left over? Be sure to show your work.

A   4

B   8

C   12

D   16

Name_____

Common Core Standard 6.NS.B.4 – The Number System

☐ John arranged mini cars in packs of 8 cars. Marsha arranged dolls in packs of 5 dolls. The total number of mini cars is identical to the total number of dolls. What is the least possible number of mini cars? Be sure to show your work.

    A   10

    B   16

    C   20

    D   40

Common Core Standard 6.NS.B.4 – The Number System

☐ Which of the following is equal to the problem below?

$$56 - 70$$

    A $14 (4 - 5)$

    B $14 (4 - 70)$

    C $14 (56 - 5)$

    D $14 (56 - 70)$

Common Core Standard 6.NS.B.4 – The Number System

☐ Vladimir has 64 coins of 25 cents and 56 coins of 50 cents. What is the greatest number of identical packs of coins with no coins left over? Be sure to show your work.

    A   4

    B   8

    C   16

    D   32

Name_____

Common Core Standard 6.NS.C.5 – The Number System

☐   Which of the following days was the coldest?

Day	Monday	Tuesday	Wednesday	Thursday
Temperature	-4°C	-8°C	-6°C	-12°C

A   Monday

B   Tuesday

C   Wednesday

D   Thursday

Common Core Standard 6.NS.C.5 – The Number System

☐   Which of the following best represents the sentence below?

"Peter owes $40"

A $40

B   -$40

C $0

D $80

Common Core Standard 6.NS.C.5 – The Number System

☐   A bird is 50 m above the sea level, and a fish is 30 m below the sea level. Which of the following numbers shows the position of fish? Be sure to show your work.

A   50 m

B   -50 m

C   30 m

D   -30 m

Common Core Standard 6.NS.C.5 – The Number System

☐ Temperature in the morning was $-2^{o}C$, and in the afternoon temperature was $7^{o}C$. What was the temperature change? Be sure to show your work.

A   5° C

B   9° C

C   -5° C

D   -9° C

Common Core Standard 6.NS.C.5 – The Number System

☐ Which of the following shows Sonia's earnings?

"Sonia earned $300 in 10 days"

A $300

B   10

C   -$300

D   -10

Common Core Standard 6.NS.C.5 – The Number System

☐ Edgar scored 200 points in a video game in the 1st level. In the 2nd level he lost 300 points. Which of the following shows his current score? Be sure to show your work.

A   500

B   100

C   0

D   -100

Common Core Standard 6.NS.C.5 – The Number System

☐ Temperature of the air changed from 72° *F* to 61° *F*. Which number represents the temperature change?   Be sure to show your work.

A   133° *F*

B   -133° *F*

C   11° *F*

D   -11° *F*

Common Core Standard 6.NS.C.5 – The Number System

☐ Which of the following represents the sentence below?

"The submarine is 300 m below the sea"

A   -300 m

B   -150 m

C   150 m

D   300 m

Common Core Standard 6.NS.C.5 – The Number System

☐ Melissa opened a bank account and deposited $500. Which of the following numbers shows the balance of her bank account?   Be sure to show your work.

A   -$500

B $500

C   -$250

D $250

Name_____

Common Core Standard 6.NS.C.5 – The Number System

☐ **A man is swimming in the sea. Which number represents his position according to the sea level? Be sure to show your work.**

A   -2 meters

B   0 meters

C   2 meters

D   20 meters

Common Core Standard 6.NS.C.5 – The Number System

☐ **Which of the following numbers represents the sentence below?**

"adding 6 strawberries to the plate"

A   1

B   -1

C   6

D   -6

Common Core Standard 6.NS.C.5 – The Number System

☐ **Niseem owes $50 to the bank. He deposited $30. Which of the following numbers shows Joshua's balance on the balance statement? Be sure to show your work.**

A $80

B $20

C   -$20

D   -$80

Name_____

Common Core Standard 6.NS.C.5 – The Number System

☐ **Allison has no money in her wallet. Which number represents this scenario? Be sure to show your work.**

A   -$100

B   -$50

C   -$25

D $0

Common Core Standard 6.NS.C.5 – The Number System

☐ **Which of the following numbers represents the sentence below?**

"Ani loses 2 lb every week"

A   2 lb

B   -2 lb

C   0 lb

D   -4 lb

Common Core Standard 6.NS.C.5 – The Number System

☐ **A building stands 20 m above the sea level, and a corral is 15 m below the sea level. What is the vertical distance between the building and the corral?**

A   5 m

B   -5 m

C   35 m

D   -35 m

Common Core Standard 6.NS.C.5 – The Number System

☐ The temperature in the afternoon was 5° C, and at night it dropped to - 1° C. What was the temperature change? Be sure to show your work.

A   - 4° C

B   4 ° C

C   - 6 ° C

D   6 ° C

Common Core Standard 6.NS.C.5 – The Number System

☐ Which of the following numbers represents scenario below?

"Hasmik added 3 apples to the bag"

A   3

B   -3

C   0

D   -1

Common Core Standard 6.NS.C.5 – The Number System

☐ Zander is standing on the rock 150 ft above the sea level, and a seabed is 150 ft below the sea level. Which number shows the middle of the vertical distance between Zander and the seabed? Be sure to show your work.

A   -150 ft

B   0 ft

C   150 ft

D   300 ft

Common Core Standard 6.NS.C.5 – The Number System

☐ The plane is flying at the altitude of 8,000 ft. If the plane changes its altitude to 6,000 ft, which number shows the change in altitude? Be sure to show your work.

A   -2000 ft

B   2000 ft

C   60000 ft

D   -6000 ft

Common Core Standard 6.NS.C.5 – The Number System

☐ Which of the following numbers represents scenario below?

"3 players are removed from the team"

A   3

B   1

C   -1

D   -3

Common Core Standard 6.NS.C.5 – The Number System

☐ Temperature changed from - 12° C to - 8° C. Which number shows the temperature change? Be sure to show your work.

A   - 20 ° C

B   - 4 ° C

C   4 ° C

D   20 ° C

Name_____

Common Core Standard 6.NS.C.5 – The Number System

☐ The submarine is 1,000 ft below the sea level. If it changes its position to 800 ft below the sea level, which number represents the change of depth? Be sure to show your work.

A   - 800 ft

B   - 200 ft

C   200 ft

D   800 ft

Common Core Standard 6.NS.C.5 – The Number System

☐ Which number represents the scenario below?

"8 soldiers are added to the platoon"

A   - 8

B   0

C   4

D   8

Common Core Standard 6.NS.C.5 – The Number System

☐ The balance on Julia's bank account was −$150. She deposited $100 to her bank account. Which number represents the new balance on her bank account? Be sure to show your work.

A   - $250

B   - $50

C $100

D $250

Common Core Standard 6.NS.C.6.A – The Number System

☐ **Which number on a number line is at the same distance from 0 as -5?**

A   -10

B   0

C   5

D   10

Common Core Standard 6.NS.C.6.A – The Number System

☐ **What is the opposite number of 6?**

A   -6

B   0

C   6

D   9

Common Core Standard 6.NS.C.6.A – The Number System

☐ **A bee is flying to the opposite number on the number line below. What is that number?**

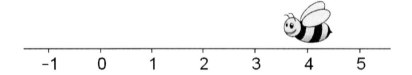
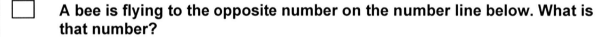

A   0

B   -4

C   -8

D   -44

Name_____

Common Core Standard 6.NS.C.6.A – The Number System

☐ **Temperature in New York at 5 A.M. was – 4 ° C, and at the same time, temperature in Sao Paulo was represented with the opposite number. What was the temperature in Sao Paulo?**

A   - 8° C

B   - 4° C

C   0° C

D   4° C

Common Core Standard 6.NS.C.6.A – The Number System

☐ **What is the opposite number of 0?**

A   0

B   any negative number

C   any positive number

D   neither of the above

Common Core Standard 6.NS.C.6.A – The Number System

☐ **A cat and a mouse are on the opposite sides of 0 on the number line below. Which number represents position of the mouse?**

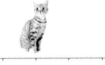

-3

A   -6

B   0

C   3

D   6

Common Core Standard 6.NS.C.6.A – The Number System

The balance on Kevan's bank account in February was $235. In October the balance on his bank account was represented with the opposite number. What was the balance on Kevan's bank account in October?

A $532

B $235

C   -$235

D   -$532

Common Core Standard 6.NS.C.6.A – The Number System

What is the opposite number of the opposite number of 8?

A   -8

B   -4

C   4

D   8

Common Core Standard 6.NS.C.6.A – The Number System

An ant is going to the opposite number on the number line below. What is that number?

-2

A   -4

B   0

C   2

D   4

Common Core Standard 6.NS.C.6.A – The Number System

☐ A kite is flying 12 m above the sea level. The position of a dolphin in the sea is represented with the opposite number. Which number represents the position of the dolphin in the sea?

A   -21 meters

B   -12 meters

C   12 meters

D   21 meters

Common Core Standard 6.NS.C.6.A – The Number System

☐ What is the opposite number of the opposite number of -17?

A   71

B   -71

C   17

D   -17

Common Core Standard 6.NS.C.6.A – The Number System

☐ The positions of a grasshopper and a June bug are represented with opposite numbers. Which number represents the position of the June bug?

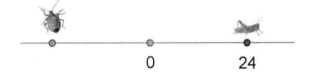

A   -42

B   -24

C   24

D   42

Common Core Standard 6.NS.C.6.A – The Number System

[ ]   Jose scored 85 points in a video game. Maria's score is represented with the opposite number. How many points did Maria score in a video game?

A   -85

B   -58

C   58

D   85

Common Core Standard 6.NS.C.6.A – The Number System

[ ]   What is the opposite number of the opposite number of 0?

A   0

B   any negative number

C   any positive number

D   neither of the above

Common Core Standard 6.NS.C.6.A – The Number System

[ ]   The positions of a pig and a hen are represented with the opposite numbers. Which number represents the position of the hen?

-34   0

A   -43

B   -34

C   34

D   42

Common Core Standard 6.NS.C.6.A – The Number System

☐ **What is the sum of 10 and its opposite number?**

A   -10

B   0

C   10

D   20

Common Core Standard 6.NS.C.6.A – The Number System

☐ **Which temperature is opposite to -12° C?**

A   -21° C

B   -12° C

C   12° C

D   21° C

Common Core Standard 6.NS.C.6.A – The Number System

☐ **The ball is thrown to the opposite number on the number line. What is that number?**

14

A   41

B   14

C   -14

D   -41

Common Core Standard 6.NS.C.6.A – The Number System

☐ **What is the difference of 12 and its opposite number?**

A   -24

B   -12

C   0

D   24

Common Core Standard 6.NS.C.6.A – The Number System

☐ **Which balance on the bank account is opposite to -$75?**

A   -$57

B $57

C $75

D $150

Common Core Standard 6.NS.C.6.A – The Number System

☐ **The positions of an elephant and a mouse are represented with the opposite numbers. Judging from the position of the elephant, which number should represent the position of the mouse?**

0

A   0

B   10

C   -10

D   101

Common Core Standard 6.NS.C.6.A – The Number System

☐ **Anthony and Andrew have opposite scores in the quiz. If Andrew scored 12 points, how many points did Anthony score?**

A -21

B -12

C 12

D 21

Common Core Standard 6.NS.C.6.A – The Number System

☐ **What is the product of -4 and its opposite number?**

A -16

B -1

C 1

D 16

Common Core Standard 6.NS.C.6.A – The Number System

☐ **A kangaroo is jumping to the opposite number on the number line. What is that number?**

-24

A -48

B 0

C 24

D 48

Name_____

Common Core Standard 6.NS.C.6.B – The Number System

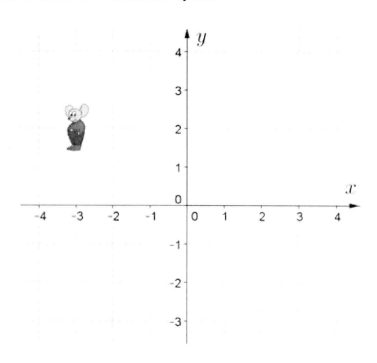

☐ **What is the position of the mouse in the coordinate plane?**

A   (-3,2)   C   (-2,3)

B   (3,-2)   D   (2,-3)

Common Core Standard 6.NS.C.6.B – The Number System

☐ **In which quadrant is the mouse in?**

A   I   C   III

B   II   D   IV

Common Core Standard 6.NS.C.6.B – The Number System

☐ **What is the position of the mouse if reflected across x-axis?**

A   (3,2)   C   (-3,2)

B   (3,-2)   D   (-3,-2)

Common Core Standard 6.NS.C.6.B – The Number System

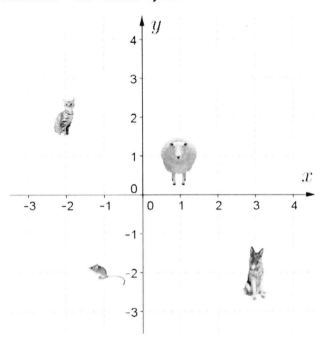

Which animal is at (3,-2) in the coordinate plane?

A   Cat   C   Mouse

B   Dog   D   Sheep

Common Core Standard 6.NS.C.6.B – The Number System

Which animal is in the III quadrant?

A   Cat   C   Mouse

B   Dog   D   Sheep

Common Core Standard 6.NS.C.6.B – The Number System

Which animal is reflected across y-axis into (-1,1)?

A   Cat   C   Mouse

B   Dog   D   Sheep

Common Core Standard 6.NS.C.6.B – The Number System

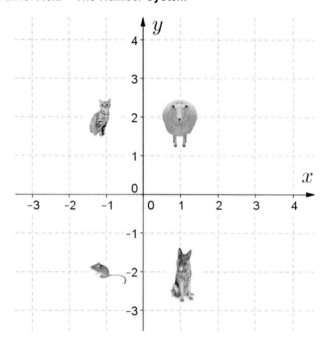

☐ By which transformation are the locations of the cat and the dog related?

A   reflection across x-axis   C   reflection across the origin

B   reflection across y-axis   D   identity

Common Core Standard 6.NS.C.6.B – The Number System

☐ By which transformation are the locations of the cat and themouse related?

A   reflection across x-axis   C   reflection across the origin

B   reflection across y-axis   D   identity

Common Core Standard 6.NS.C.6.B – The Number System

☐ By which transformation are the locations of the mouse and the dog related?

A   reflection across x-axis   C   reflection across the origin

B   reflection across y-axis   D   identity

Name_____

Common Core Standard 6.NS.C.6.B – The Number System

☐   **By which transformation are points A(x,y) and B(-x,-y) related?**

A   reflection across x-axis

B   reflection across y-axis

C   reflection across the origin

D   reflection across point (1,1)

Common Core Standard 6.NS.C.6.B – The Number System

☐   **By which transformation are points A(x,y) and B(-x,y) related?**

A   reflection across x-axis

B   reflection across y-axis

C   reflection across the origin

D   reflection across point (1,1)

Common Core Standard 6.NS.C.6.B – The Number System

☐   **By which transformation are points A(x,y) and B(x,-y) related?**

A   reflection across x-axis

B   reflection across y-axis

C   reflection across the origin

D   reflection across point (1,1)

Common Core Standard 6.NS.C.6.B – The Number System

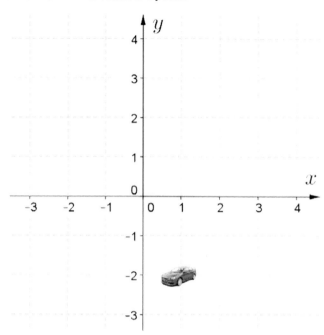

What is the position of the car in the coordinate plane?

A   (1,2)   C   (-1,2)

B   (1,-2)   D   (-1,-2)

Common Core Standard 6.NS.C.6.B – The Number System

In which quadrant is the car in?

A   I   C   III

B   II   D   IV

Common Core Standard 6.NS.C.6.B – The Number System

What is the position of the car if reflected across y-axis?

A   (1,2)   C   (-1,2)

B   (1,-2)   D   (-1,-2)

Common Core Standard 6.NS.C.6.B – The Number System

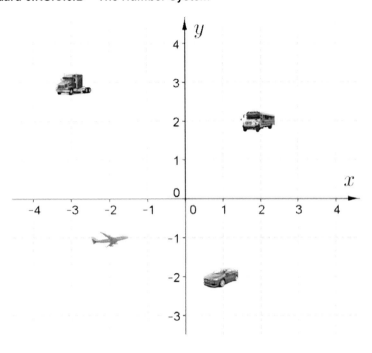

Which vehicle is at (2,2) in the coordinate plane?

A   Airplane   C   Truck

B   Car   D   Bus

Common Core Standard 6.NS.C.6.B – The Number System

Which vehicle is in the II quadrant?

A   Airplane   C   Truck

B   Car   D   Bus

Common Core Standard 6.NS.C.6.B – The Number System

Which vehicle is reflected across the origin from the point (2,1)?

A   Airplane   C   Truck

B   Car   D   Bus

Common Core Standard 6.NS.C.6.B – The Number System

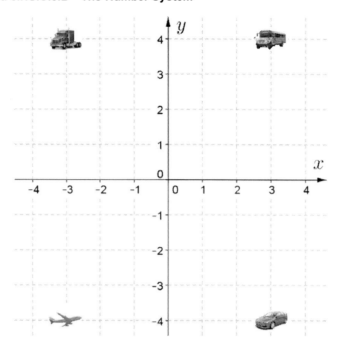

☐ Which two vehicles have the same coordinates with opposite signs?

A   Airplane and Bus   C   Truck and Airplane

B   Car and Airplane   D   Bus and Truck

Common Core Standard 6.NS.C.6.B – The Number System

☐ Which two vehicles have the same coordinates with the opposite signs of x-coordinates?

A   Airplane and Truck   C   Truck and Car

B   Car and Airplane   D   Bus and Car

Common Core Standard 6.NS.C.6.B – The Number System

☐ Which two vehicles have the same coordinates with the opposite signs of y-coordinates?

A   Airplane and Bus   C   Truck and Car

B   Car and Airplane   D   Bus and Car

Common Core Standard 6.NS.C.6.B – The Number System

☐ **Referring to the same picture on the previous page, which transformation changes the sign of the x-coordinate of the point P(2,3) in the coordinate plane?**

A   reflection across x-axis

B   reflection across y-axis

C   reflection across the origin

D   reflection across the point P(2,3)

Common Core Standard 6.NS.C.6.B – The Number System

☐ **In which quadrant is the point with both coordinates negative?**

A   I

B   II

C   III

D   IV

Common Core Standard 6.NS.C.6.B – The Number System

☐ **If the point P(x,y) is in the I quadrant then:**

A $x>0, y>0$

B $x<0, y>0$

C $x>0, y<0$

D $x<0, y<0$

Common Core Standard 6.NS.C.6.C – The Number System

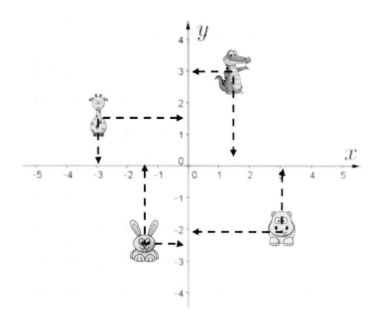

What is the position of alligator in the coordinate plane?

A   (-3, 3/2)   C   (3, -2)

B   (-3/2, -5/2)   D   (3/2, 3)

Common Core Standard 6.NS.C.6.C – The Number System

Which cartoon character is located at (-3/2, -5/2)?

A   Giraffe   C   Hippopotamus

B   Rabbit   D   Alligator

Common Core Standard 6.NS.C.6.C – The Number System

Which Disney character is located in II quadrant?

A   Giraffe   C   Hippoptamus

B   Rabbit   D   Alligator

Common Core Standard 6.NS.C.6.C – The Number System

0   1

What is the position of Mickey Mouse on the number line?

A   7   C   3/10

B   7/10   D   3

Common Core Standard 6.NS.C.6.C – The Number System

Which character is located at 4/10?

A   Giraffe   C   Rabbit

B   Hippopotamus   D   Alligator

Common Core Standard 6.NS.C.6.C – The Number System

Which two characters are 0.4 units distant?

A   Giraffe and Alligator   C   Rabbit and Hippopotamus

B   Hippopotamus and Alligator   D   Rabbit and Alligator

Name_____

Common Core Standard 6.NS.C.6.C – The Number System

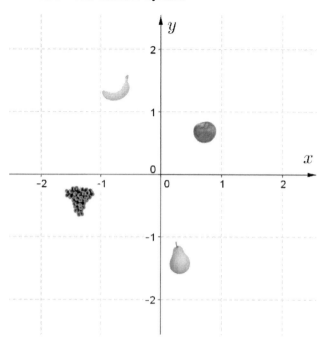

□ What is the possible position of the grapes in the coordinate plane?

A   (-4/3, -1/2)   C   (3/4, 3/4)

B   (-2/3, 4/3)   D   (1/3, -4/3)

Common Core Standard 6.NS.C.6.C – The Number System

□ Which fruit is the closest to (1/2, -3/2)?

A   Banana   C   Pear

B   Grapes   D   Apple

Common Core Standard 6.NS.C.6.C – The Number System

□ Which fruit is located in I quadrant?

A   Banana   C   Pear

B   Grapes   D   Apple

Common Core Standard 6.NS.C.6.C – The Number System

0   1

☐ **What is the position of the banana on the number line?**

A   -0.2   C   -2/5

B   2/5   D   0.2

Common Core Standard 6.NS.C.6.C – The Number System

☐ **Which fruit is located at 4/5?**

A   Pear   C   Grapes

B   Banana   D   Apple

Common Core Standard 6.NS.C.6.C – The Number System

☐ **Which two fruits are 0.6 units distant?**

A   Pear and Banana   C   Grapes and Apple

B   Banana and Grapes   D   Apple and Banana

Name_____

Common Core Standard 6.NS.C.6.C – The Number System

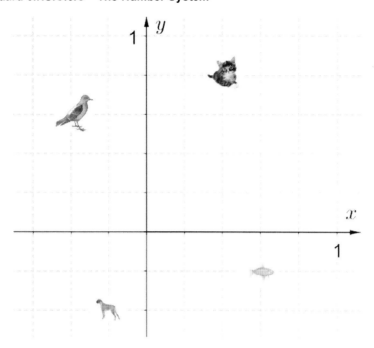

☐ **What is the position of the bird in the coordinate plane?**

A   (-0.2, 0.3)   C   (-2/5, 3/5)

B   (0.2, 0.3)   D   (2/5, 3/5)

Common Core Standard 6.NS.C.6.C – The Number System

☐ **Which animal is located at (3/5, -1/5)?**

A   Bird   C   Dog

B   Cat   D   Fish

Common Core Standard 6.NS.C.6.C – The Number System

☐ **Which animal is located in III quadrant?**

A   Bird   C   Dog

B   Cat   D   Fish

Common Core Standard 6.NS.C.6.C – The Number System

0   1

☐ **What is the position of the fish on the number line?**

A   2   C   1/4

B   1/2   D   2/2

Common Core Standard 6.NS.C.6.C – The Number System

☐ **Which animal is located at -0.75?**

A   Cat   C   Dog

B   Bird   D   Fish

Common Core Standard 6.NS.C.6.C – The Number System

☐ **Which two animals are 1.25 units distant?**

A   Bird and Fish   C   Fish and Dog

B   Cat and Dog   D   Bird and Cat

Name_____

Common Core Standard 6.NS.C.6.C – The Number System

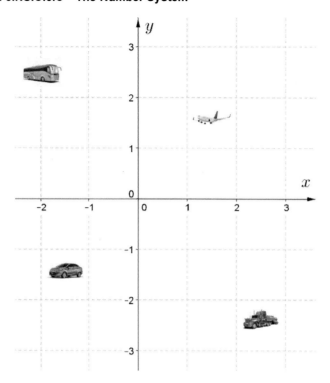

☐   **What is the possible position of the bus in the coordinate plane?**

A   (-2, 5/2)   C   (2.5, -2.5)

B   (-3/2, -3/2)   D   (1.5, 1.5)

Common Core Standard 6.NS.C.6.C – The Number System

☐   **Which vehicle is the closest to (-1.5, -1.5)?**

A   Bus   C   Truck

B   Airplane   D   Car

Common Core Standard 6.NS.C.6.C – The Number System

☐   **Which vehicle is located in IV quadrant?**

A   Bus   C   Truck

B   Airplane   D   Car

Common Core Standard 6.NS.C.6.C – The Number System

0   1

What is the position of the truck on the number line?

A   -1   C   -1/3

B   1   D   1/3

Common Core Standard 6.NS.C.6.C – The Number System

Which vehicle is located at 4/3?

A   Car   C   Bus

B   Truck   D   Airplane

Common Core Standard 6.NS.C.6.C – The Number System

Which two vehicles are 1 unit distant?

A   Car and Truck   C   Bus and Airplane

B   Truck and Bus   D   Airplane and Car

Common Core Standard 6.NS.C.7.A– The Number System

☐ **Which temperature is greater than the temperature represented by the point on the number line below?**

A   -6° C

B   -5° C

C   1° C

D   4° C

Common Core Standard 6.NS.C.7.A– The Number System

☐ **Which number is located to the left from -2 on the number line?**

A   -1

B   0

C   -3

D   3

Common Core Standard 6.NS.C.7.A– The Number System

☐ **On which side from 8 on the number line is x, if x < 8?**

A   Left

B   Right

C   Up

D   Down

Common Core Standard 6.NS.C.7.A– The Number System

☐ **Which balance on the bank account is greater than the balance represented by the point on the number line below?**

0   100

A   -$600

B   -$700

C   -$200

D   -$400

Common Core Standard 6.NS.C.7.A– The Number System

☐ **Which number is located to the right from 12 on the number line?**

A   18

B   8

C   -8

D   -18

Common Core Standard 6.NS.C.7.A– The Number System

☐ **On which side from -1 on the number line is x, if x > -1?**

A   Left

B   Right

C   Up

D   Down

Common Core Standard 6.NS.C.7.A– The Number System

☐ **Which altitude is lower than the altitude represented by the point on the number line below?**

0   500

A   3,000

B   2,500

C   2,000

D   1,500

Common Core Standard 6.NS.C.7.A– The Number System

☐ **Which number is located to the left from 5 on the number line?**

A   55

B   6

C   5

D   3

Common Core Standard 6.NS.C.7.A– The Number System

☐ **On which side from 9 on the number line is x, if x > 9?**

A   Left

B   Right

C   Up

D   Down

Common Core Standard 6.NS.C.7.A– The Number System

☐ **Which score in the quiz is lower than the score represented by the point on the number line below?**

0   10

A   -40

B   40

C   -60

D   60

Common Core Standard 6.NS.C.7.A– The Number System

☐ **Which number is located to the right from -14 on the number line?**

A   -13

B   -14

C   -15

D   -16

Common Core Standard 6.NS.C.7.A– The Number System

☐ **On which side from -10 on the number line is x, if x < -10?**

A   Left

B   Right

C   Up

D   Down

Common Core Standard 6.NS.C.7.A– The Number System

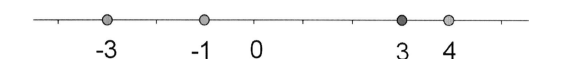

☐ **What is the greatest number on the number line above?**

A   -3

B   -1

C   3

D   4

Common Core Standard 6.NS.C.7.A– The Number System

☐ **What is the least number on the number line above?**

A   0

B   -1

C   -3

D   4

Common Core Standard 6.NS.C.7.A– The Number System

☐ **Look at the number line above. Which of the following inequalities is true?**

A   -1 < -3

B   -1 > -3

C   3 < -1

D   -3 > 4

Common Core Standard 6.NS.C.7.A– The Number System

-7   -4 -3   -1

☐   **What is the greatest number on the number line above?**

A   -1

B   -3

C   -4

D   -7

Common Core Standard 6.NS.C.7.A– The Number System

☐   **What is the least number on the number line above?**

A   -1

B   -3

C   -4

D   -7

Common Core Standard 6.NS.C.7.A– The Number System

☐   **Look at the number line above. Which of the following inequalities is true?**

A   -1 < -7

B   -3 > -4

C   -3 < -4

D   -4 > -1

Common Core Standard 6.NS.C.7.A– The Number System

☐   **Look at the number line below. Which inequality is true?**

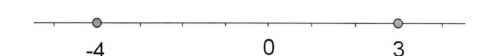

-4   0   3

A   -4 < 3

B   -4 > 3

C   3 < -4

D   -3 > 4

Common Core Standard 6.NS.C.7.A– The Number System

☐   **Which inequality is represented by the number line below?**

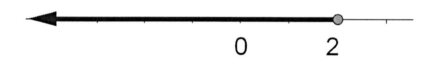

0   2

A   x > 2

B   x > 0

C   x < 2

D   s < 0

Common Core Standard 6.NS.C.7.A– The Number System

☐   **If x is on the left side from -4 on the number line then:**

A   x > -4

B   x < -4

C   x > 0

D   x < 4

Name_____

Common Core Standard 6.NS.C.7.A– The Number System

☐　**Look at the number line below. Which inequality is true?**

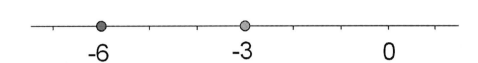

A　　-3 < -6

B　　-3 > -6

C　　-6 > -3

D　　6 < 3

Common Core Standard 6.NS.C.7.A– The Number System

☐　**Which inequality is represented by the number line below?**

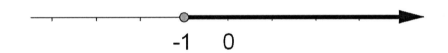

A　　x > -1

B　　x < -1

C　　x > 0

D　　x < 0

Common Core Standard 6.NS.C.7.A– The Number System

☐　**If x is on the right side from 7 on the number line then:**

A　　x > -7

B　　x < -7

C　　x > 7

D　　x < 7

Common Core Standard 6.NS.C.7.B– The Number System

City	New York	Tokyo	Paris	Sydney
Temperature	-4° C	-6°C	-2°C	-7°C

☐ **Look at the table above. Which city is the warmest?**

A   New York

B   Tokyo

C   Paris

D   Sydney

Common Core Standard 6.NS.C.7.B– The Number System

☐ **Which city is the coldest?**

A   New York

B   Tokyo

C   Paris

D   Sydney

Common Core Standard 6.NS.C.7.B– The Number System

☐ **Which city is 2° *C* colder than New York?**

A   Sydney

B   Tokyo

C   Paris

D   Neither of the above

Common Core Standard 6.NS.C.7.B– The Number System

Object	Airplane	Fish	Submarine	Bird
Altitude	10,000 ft	-20 ft	-500 ft	100 ft

☐ Look at the table above. Which object is the highest?

A   Airplane

B   Fish

C   Submarine

D   Bird

Common Core Standard 6.NS.C.7.B– The Number System

☐ Which object is the deepest?

A   Airplane

B   Fish

C   Submarine

D   Bird

Common Core Standard 6.NS.C.7.B– The Number System

☐ Which two objects are below the sea level?

A   Airplane and Fish

B   Fish and Submarine

C   Submarine and Bird

D   Bird and Airplane

Common Core Standard 6.NS.C.7.B– The Number System

Name	John	Sarah	Peter	Mia
Bank Account Balance	-$30	$20	-$50	$40

☐ Look at the table above. Who has the greatest amount of money?

A   John

B   Sarah

C   Peter

D   Mia

Common Core Standard 6.NS.C.7.B– The Number System

☐ Who has the greatest debt?

A   John

B   Sarah

C   Peter

D   Mia

Common Core Standard 6.NS.C.7.B– The Number System

☐ Who has $10 more than John?

A   Sarah

B   Peter

C   Mia

D   None of the above

Common Core Standard 6.NS.C.7.B– The Number System

Player	Ella	Jack	Anna	Ryan
Video Game Points	200	-10	150	-150

☐ Look at the table above. Who has the best score?

A Ella

B Jack

C Anna

D Ryan

Common Core Standard 6.NS.C.7.B– The Number System

☐ Who has the worst score?

A Ella

B Jack

C Anna

D Ryan

Common Core Standard 6.NS.C.7.B– The Number System

☐ Who scored 50 points less than Ella?

A Jack

B Anna

C Ryan

D None of the above

Name_____

Common Core Standard 6.NS.C.7.B– The Number System

Fruit	Apple	Pear	Orange	Apricot
Weight (lb)	1/4	0.30	1/3	0.20

☐ **Look at the table above. Which fruit is the heaviest?**

A   Apple

B   Pear

C   Orange

D   Apricot

Common Core Standard 6.NS.C.7.B– The Number System

☐ **Which fruit is the lightest?**

A   Apple

B   Pear

C   Orange

D   Apricot

Common Core Standard 6.NS.C.7.B– The Number System

☐ **Order fruits from lightest to heaviest.**

A   Apple, Pear, Orange, Apricot

B   Apricot, Apple, Pear, Orange

C   Pear, Apple, Orange, Apricot

D   Orange, Pear, Apple, Apricot

Common Core Standard 6.NS.C.7.B– The Number System

Vehicle	Car	Truck	Motorbike	Bicycle
Weight (tons)	1.2	3 1/2	0.2	1/50

☐ Look at the table above. Which vehicle is the heaviest?

A   Car

B   Truck

C   Motorbike

D   Bicycle

Common Core Standard 6.NS.C.7.B– The Number System

☐   Which vehicle is the lightest?

A   Car

B   Truck

C   Motorbike

D   Bicycle

Common Core Standard 6.NS.C.7.B– The Number System

☐   Order vehicles from heaviest to lightest.

A   Car, Truck, Motorbike, Bicycle

B   Bicycle, Motorbike, Truck, Car

C   Bicycle, Motorbike, Car, Truck

D   Truck, Car, Motorbike, Bicycle

Name_____

Common Core Standard 6.NS.C.7.B– The Number System

Day	Monday	Tuesday	Wednesday	Thursday
Water Level (Meters)	0.4	-0.2	1/2	-1/4

☐ Look at the table above. On which day was the level of water the highest?

A   Monday

B   Tuesday

C   Wednesday

D   Thursday

Common Core Standard 6.NS.C.7.B– The Number System

☐ On which day was the level of water the lowest?

A   Monday

B   Tuesday

C   Wednesday

D   Thursday

Common Core Standard 6.NS.C.7.B– The Number System

☐ Order levels of water from lowest to highest.

A   -0.2, -1/4, 0.4, 1/2

B   -1/4, -0.2, 0.4, 1/2

C   1/2, 0.4, -0.2, -1/4

D   0.4, 1/2, -1/4, -0.2

Name_____

Common Core Standard 6.NS.C.7.B– The Number System

Animal	Cat	Dog	Sheep	Hen
Height (Yards)	1/4	0.7	0.83	1/3

☐ Look at the table above. Which animal is the tallest?

A   Cat

B   Dog

C   Sheep

D   Hen

Common Core Standard 6.NS.C.7.B– The Number System

☐ Which animal is the shortest?

A   Cat

B   Dog

C   Sheep

D   Hen

Common Core Standard 6.NS.C.7.B– The Number System

☐ Order animals from tallest to shortest.

A   Cat, Dog, Sheep, Hen

B   Hen, Sheep, Dog, Cat

C   Cat, Hen, Dog, Sheep

D   Sheep, Dog, Hen, Cat

Common Core Standard 6.NS.C.7.C– The Number System

☐ Anthony's balance on the bank account is -$52. What is the size of his debt?

A   -$52

B   -$25

C $25

D $52

Common Core Standard 6.NS.C.7.C– The Number System

☐ What is the absolute value of 76.4?

A   76.4

B   67.4

C   -67.4

D   -76.4

Common Core Standard 6.NS.C.7.C– The Number System

☐ The altitude of the fish is -21 ft. How deep is the fish in the sea?

A   -12 ft

B   12 ft

C   -21 ft

D   21 ft

Name_____

Common Core Standard 6.NS.C.7.C– The Number System

☐ What temperature in the table below is 13 degrees below zero on the Celsius scale?

Temperature	13°C	31°C	-13°C	-31°C

A   13° C

B   31° C

C   -13° C

D   -31° C

Common Core Standard 6.NS.C.7.C– The Number System

☐ Fill in the missing number.

$$-34 = |\quad|$$

A   -43

B   43

C   -34

D   34

Common Core Standard 6.NS.C.7.C– The Number System

☐ Which of the following numbers has the greatest absolute value?

A   -2/3

B   -3/2

C   4/3

D   3/4

Name_____

Common Core Standard 6.NS.C.7.C– The Number System

☐ **Order debtors according to their debts from least to greatest.**

Debtor	Maya	Jordan	Layla
Account Balance	-$50	-$70	-$60

A   Maya, Jordan, Layla

B   Layla, Jordan, Maya

C   Jordan, Layla, Maya

D   Maya, Layla, Peter

Common Core Standard 6.NS.C.7.C– The Number System

☐ **What is the absolute value of -5/8?**

A   -5/8

B   -8/5

C   5/8

D   8/5

Common Core Standard 6.NS.C.7.C– The Number System

☐ **Order animals according to their depths from greatest to least.**

Animal	Fish	Dolphin	Octopus
Depth	-20 ft	-50 ft	-30 ft

A   Dolphin, Octopus, Fish

B   Fish, Octopus, Dolphin

C   Octopus, Dolphin, Fish

D   Fish, Dolphin, Octopus

Name_____

Common Core Standard 6.NS.C.7.C– The Number System

☐ Order cities according to the absolute values of temperatures from least to greatest.

City	Paris	London	Rome	Berlin
Temperature	-5°C	1°C	-3°C	6°C

A   Paris, London, Rome, Berlin

B   Berlin, Paris, Rome, London

C   Paris, Rome, London, Berlin

D   London, Rome, Paris, Berlin

Common Core Standard 6.NS.C.7.C– The Number System

☐ Fill in the missing number.

$$\_\_\_ = |-8.2|$$

A   8.2

B   -2.8

C   -8.2

D   2.8

Common Core Standard 6.NS.C.7.C– The Number System

☐ Which of the following numbers has the least absolute value?

A   -3/5

B   5/3

C   -4/9

D   9/4

Common Core Standard 6.NS.C.7.C– The Number System

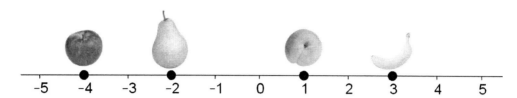

Look at the number line above. Which fruit is at the position with the greatest absolute value?

A   Apple

B   Pear

C   Apricot

D   Banana

Common Core Standard 6.NS.C.7.C– The Number System

Which fruit is at the position with the least absolute value?

A   Apple

B   Pear

C   Apricot

D   Banana

Common Core Standard 6.NS.C.7.C– The Number System

What is the sum of absolute values of positions of apple and apricot?

A   -5

B   -3

C   3

D   5

Name_____

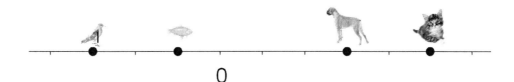

0

☐   Look at the number line above. Which animal is at the position with the greatest absolute value?

A   Bird

B   Fish

C   Dog

D   Cat

☐   Which animal is at the position with the least absolute value?

A   Bird

B   Fish

C   Dog

D   Cat

☐   Which two animals have the difference of absolute values of positions equal to zero?

A   Bird and Fish

B   Fish and Cat

C   Dog and Cat

D   Bird and Dog

Common Core Standard 6.NS.C.7.C– The Number System

Day	Monday	Tuesday	Wednesday	Thursday
Water Level (Meters)	-0.4	0.2	-1/2	1/4

☐ **Look at the table above. On which day was the absolute value of level of water the highest?**

A   Monday

B   Tuesday

C   Wednesday

D   Thursday

Common Core Standard 6.NS.C.7.C– The Number System

☐ **On which day was the absolute value of level of water the lowest?**

A   Monday

B   Tuesday

C   Wednesday

D   Thursday

Common Core Standard 6.NS.C.7.C– The Number System

☐ **Order absolute value of levels of water from lowest to highest.**

A |0.2|, |1/4|, |-0.4|, |-1/2|

B |1/4|, |0.2|, |0.4|, |1/2|

C |0.2|, |1/4|, |-0.4|, |-1/2|

D |-0.4|, |-1/2|, |1/4|, |0.2|

Common Core Standard 6.NS.C.7.C– The Number System

☐ **Fill in the missing sign.**

$$\left| -\frac{2}{3} \right| \underline{\qquad} | 0.5 |$$

A　=

B　>

C　<

D　≤

Common Core Standard 6.NS.C.7.C– The Number System

☐ **Order absolute values of numbers below from greatest to lowest.**

$$-3.2, \ 0.6, \ -\frac{4}{5}$$

A　|-3.2|, |-4/5|, |0.6|

B　|0.6|, |-4/5|, |-3.2|

C　|-3.2|, |0.6|, |-4/5|

D　|-4/5|, |-3.2|, |0.6|

Common Core Standard 6.NS.C.7.C– The Number System

☐ **What is the sum of absolute values of numbers in the number scale below?**

0	1	0
1	0	0
0	0	-1

A　1/3

B　-1/3

C　3

D　-2

Common Core Standard 6.NS.C.7.D– The Number System

Debtor	Emma	Ethan	Olivia	Jacob
Account Balance	-$200	-$150	-$300	-$250

Look at the table above. Who has the greatest debt?

A   Emma

B   Ethan

C   Olivia

D   Jacob

Common Core Standard 6.NS.C.7.D– The Number System

Who has the least debt?

A   Emma

B   Ethan

C   Olivia

D   Jacob

Common Core Standard 6.NS.C.7.D– The Number System

Order debtors according to debts from least to greatest.

A   Emma, Ethan, Olivia, Jacob

B   Ethan, Emma, Jacob, Olivia

C   Olivia, Jacob, Emma, Ethan

D   Jacob, Olivia, Ethan, Emma

Common Core Standard 6.NS.C.7.D– The Number System

City	Austin	Chicago	New York	Detroit
Temperature	-8°C	-5°C	-6°C	-10°C

☐ Look at the table above. Which city is the coldest?

A   Austin

B   Chicago

C   New York

D   Detroit

Common Core Standard 6.NS.C.7.D– The Number System

☐ Which city is the warmest?

A   Austin

B   Chicago

C   New York

D   Detroit

Common Core Standard 6.NS.C.7.D– The Number System

☐ Order cities according to absolute values of temperatures from greatest to least.

A   Detroit, Austin, New York, Chicago

B   Austin, Chicago, New York, Detroit

C   Detroit, New York, Chicago, Austin

D   Chicago, New York, Austin, Detroit

Common Core Standard 6.NS.C.7.D– The Number System

| -6 | -5 | -4 | -3 | -2 | -1 | 0 | 1 | 2 | 3 | 4 |

☐ **Look at the number line above. Which vehicle is at the position with the greatest absolute value?**

A   Bus

B   Airplane

C   Truck

D   Car

Common Core Standard 6.NS.C.7.D– The Number System

☐ **Which vehicle is at the position with the least absolute value?**

A   Bus

B   Airplane

C   Truck

D   Car

Common Core Standard 6.NS.C.7.D– The Number System

☐ **Which two vehicles are at the positions with equal absolute values?**

A   Bus and Airplane

B   Airplane and Truck

C   Truck and Car

D   Airplane and Car

Common Core Standard 6.NS.C.7.D– The Number System

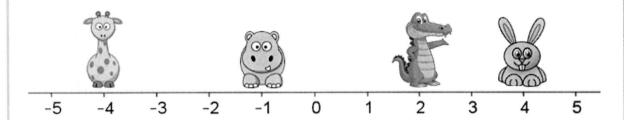

-5 -4 -3 -2 -1 0 1 2 3 4 5

☐ **Look at the number line above. Which cartoon character is at the position with greater absolute value than the absolute value of the position of the rabbit?**

A   Giraffe

B   Hippopotamus

C   Alligator

D   None of the above

Common Core Standard 6.NS.C.7.D– The Number System

☐ **Which cartoon character is at the position with lesser absolute value than the absolute value of the position of the alligator?**

A   Giraffe

B   Hippopotamus

C   Rabbit

D   None of the above

Common Core Standard 6.NS.C.7.D– The Number System

☐ **Which two cartoon characters are at the positions with equal absolute values?**

A   Giraffe and Hippopotamus

B   Hippopotamus and Alligator

C   Alligator and Rabbit

D   Rabbit and Giraffe

Common Core Standard 6.NS.C.7.D– The Number System

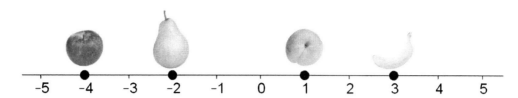

☐   **Look at the number line above. Which fruit is at the position with greater absolute value than the absolute value of the position of banana?**

A   **Apple**

B   **Pear**

C   **Apricot**

D   **None of the above**

Common Core Standard 6.NS.C.7.D– The Number System

☐   **Which fruit is at the position with lesser absolute value than the absolute value of the position of banana?**

A   **Apple and Pear**

B   **Pear and Apricot**

C   **Apricot**

D   **None of the above**

Common Core Standard 6.NS.C.7.D– The Number System

☐   **What is the product of absolute values of the positions of banana and pear?**

A   **-1**

B   **1**

C   **-6**

D   **6**

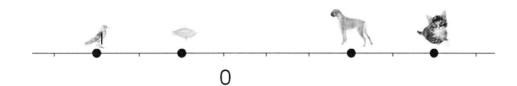

Common Core Standard 6.NS.C.7.D– The Number System

Look at the number line above. Which animals are at the position with the greater absolute value than the absolute value of the bird?

A   Fish, Dog and Cat

B   Dog and Cat

C   Fish and Dog

D   Cat

Common Core Standard 6.NS.C.7.D– The Number System

Which animals are at the position with lesser absolute value than the absolute value of the fish?

A   Bird

B   Dog and Cat

C   Bird, Dog and Cat

D   None of the above

Common Core Standard 6.NS.C.7.D– The Number System

Order animals according to the absolute values of their positions from least to greatest.

A   Bird, Fish, Dog, Cat

B   Bird, Dog, Fish, Cat

C   Fish, Bird, Dog, Cat

D   Cat, Dog, Bird, Fish,

Common Core Standard 6.NS.C.7.D– The Number System

Day	Monday	Tuesday	Wednesday	Thursday
Water Level (Meters)	-0.4	0.2	-1/2	1/4

☐ Look at the table above. On which day was the absolute value of the water level lesser than the water level on Thursday?

A   Monday

B   Tuesday

C   Wednesday

D   Thursday

Common Core Standard 6.NS.C.7.D– The Number System

☐ On which day(s) was the absolute value of the water level greater than the water level on Tuesday?

A   Thursday

B   Monday and Wednesday

C   Wednesday and Thursday

D   Monday, Wednesday and Thursday

Common Core Standard 6.NS.C.7.D– The Number System

☐ On which day was the absolute value of the water level farthest from zero?

A   Monday

B   Tuesday

C   Wednesday

D   Thursday

Common Core Standard 6.NS.C.7.D– The Number System

☐ **Fill in the missing sign.**

$$0.34 \_\_\_ \left|-\frac{2}{3}\right|$$

A   =

B   >

C   <

D   ≥

Common Core Standard 6.NS.C.7.D– The Number System

☐ **Order numbers below from greatest to lowest.**

$$\left|-\frac{3}{4}\right|, 0.7, -2$$

A |-3/4|, 0.7, -2

B   -2, 0.7, |-3/4|

C   0.7, -2, |-3/4|

D |-3/4|, -2, 0.7

Common Core Standard 6.NS.C.7.D– The Number System

☐ **What is the difference of absolute values of -0.8 and 4/5?**

A   8/5

B   -8/5

C   1

D   0

Common Core Standard 6.NS.C.8– The Number System

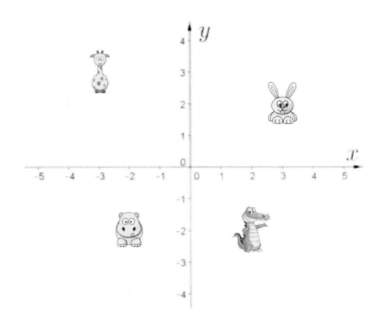

☐ **Look at the graph above. What is the position of the giraffe?**

A (3,-3) C (3,3)

B (-3,3) D (-3,-3)

Common Core Standard 6.NS.C.8– The Number System

☐ **What is the distance between the hippopotamus and the alligator?**

A 2 units C 4 units

B 3 units D 5 units

Common Core Standard 6.NS.C.8– The Number System

☐ **Which path should the alligator follow to meet the rabbit?**

A 1 unit left, 4 units up C 1 unit left, 4 units down

B 1 unit right, 4 units down D 1 unit right, 4 units up

Name_____

Common Core Standard 6.NS.C.8– The Number System

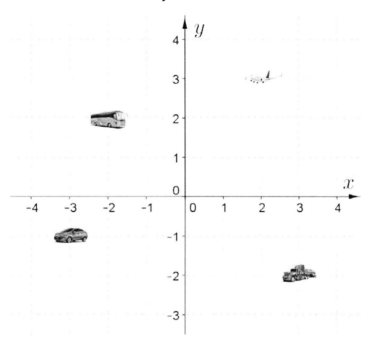

☐ Look at the graph above. Which vehicle is at (2,3)?

A	Bus		C	Airplane
B	Car		D	Truck

Common Core Standard 6.NS.C.8– The Number System

☐ Which vehicle is in III quadrant?

A	Bus		C	Airplane
B	Car		D	Truck

Common Core Standard 6.NS.C.8– The Number System

☐ The truck moves 2 units left and 3 units up. Where does it end?

A	(1,1)		C	(5,1)
B	(1,-1)		D	(5,1)

Name_____

Common Core Standard 6.NS.C.8– The Number System

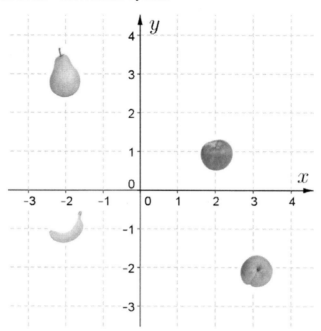

☐ Look at the graph above. What is the position of the apple?

A (1,2)   C (-1,2)

B (2,1)   D (2,-1)

Common Core Standard 6.NS.C.8– The Number System

☐ What is the distance between the banana and the pear?

A 1 unit   C 3 units

B 2 units   D 4 units

Common Core Standard 6.NS.C.8– The Number System

☐ In which quadrant is the apricot?

A I   C III

B II   D IV

Name_____

Common Core Standard 6.NS.C.8– The Number System

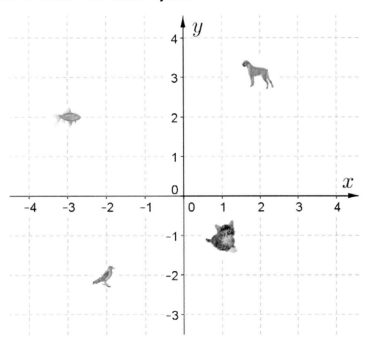

☐ **Look at the graph above. Which animal is at (-2,-2)?**

A   Fish   C   Bird

B   Dog   D   Cat

Common Core Standard 6.NS.C.8– The Number System

☐ **Which path should the cat follow to catch the fish?**

A   4 units left, 3 units up   C   4 units left, 3 units down

B   4 units right, 3 units up   D   4 units right, 3 units down

---

Common Core Standard 6.NS.C.8– The Number System

☐ **The dog moves 2 units left and 3 units down. Where does the dog end?**

A   (4,0)   C   (4,6)

B   (0,6)   D   (0,0)

Name_____

Common Core Standard 6.NS.C.8– The Number System

☐ **What is the distance between points A(-4,6) and B(-4,8)?**

    A   2

    B   4

    C   6

    D   8

Common Core Standard 6.NS.C.8– The Number System

☐ **In which quadrant is point A(3,-4)?**

    A   I

    B   II

    C   III

    D   IV

Common Core Standard 6.NS.C.8– The Number System

☐ **What is the distance between points A(2,-3) and B(-6,-3)?**

    A   2

    B   4

    C   6

    D   8

Name_____

Common Core Standard 6.NS.C.8– The Number System

☐ **Point A(-3,-5) has moved 4 units right. Where did it end?**

    A   (-7,-5)

    B   (1,-5)

    C   (-3,-9)

    D   (-3,-1)

Common Core Standard 6.NS.C.8– The Number System

☐ **Which path should point A(-1,1) move to appear in III quadrant?**

    A   3 units down

    B   3 units left

    C   3 units up

    D   3 units right

Common Core Standard 6.NS.C.8– The Number System

☐ **In which quadrant is the point with both coordinates negative?**

    A   I

    B   II

    C   III

    D   IV

Common Core Standard 6.NS.C.8– The Number System

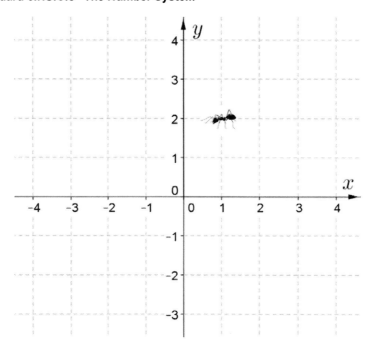

☐ **Look at the graph above. In which quadrant is the ant?**

A   I   C   III

B   II   D   IV

Common Core Standard 6.NS.C.8– The Number System

☐ **If the ant moves 3 units down, where will it end?**

A   (-2,2)   C   (1,-1)

B   (2,-2)   D   (-1,1)

Common Core Standard 6.NS.C.8– The Number System

☐ **Which path should the ant follow to end in IV quadrant?**

A   2 units left, 3 units up   C   2 units left, 3 units down

B   2 units right, 3 units down   D   2 units right, 3 units up

Name_____

Common Core Standard 6.NS.C.8– The Number System

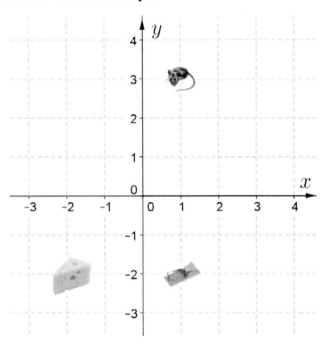

☐ **Look at the graph above. What is the position of the mouse?**

A   (3,1)   C   (-1,3)

B   (1,3)   D   (3,-1)

Common Core Standard 6.NS.C.8– The Number System

☐ **What is the distance between the cheese and the mousetrap?**

A   1 unit   C   3 units

B   2 units   D   4 units

Common Core Standard 6.NS.C.8– The Number System

☐ **Which path should the mouse follow to avoid the mousetrap and get to the cheese?**

A   3 units left, 5 units up   C   5 units down, 3 units left

B   3 units left, 5 units down   D   5 units down, 3 units right

Common Core Standard 6.EE.A.1 – Expressions & Equations

☐ **Mary had a cake. She cut the cake in 2 equal pieces. Then she halved each piece and so on. She repeated this process 5 times. How many pieces of cake did she get? Be sure to show your work.**

    A 2^5

    B 5^2

    C 2^2

    D 5^5

Common Core Standard 6.EE.A.1 – Expressions & Equations

☐ **Write as an exponent for the problem below.**

2 x 2 x 2

    A 2^2

    B 3^3

    C 2^3

    D 3^2

Common Core Standard 6.EE.A.1 – Expressions & Equations

☐ **Marty cut a stick in 3 equal pieces. Then he cut each piece in 3 equal pieces and so on. He repeated this process 4 times. How many pieces did he get? Be sure to show your work.**

    A 4^4

    B 3^3

    C 4^3

    D 3^4

Common Core Standard 6.EE.A.1 – Expressions & Equations

Lilly had 8 lb of rice. She divided it in 4 equal amounts. Then she divided each amount of rice in 4 equal amounts and so on. She repeated this process 4 times. How many equal amounts of rice did Lilly get? Be sure to show your work.

A 4^4

B 4^3

C 4^8

D 8^4

Common Core Standard 6.EE.A.1 – Expressions & Equations

Solve the expression below to find the correct answer. Be sure to show your work.

$$4^3$$

A   7

B   12

C   27

D   64

Common Core Standard 6.EE.A.1 – Expressions & Equations

Alexander divided equally 5 lb of popcorn in 3 bags. Then he divided each bag of popcorn in 3 equal smaller bags and so on. He repeated this process 5 times. How many small bags of popcorn did he get? Be sure to show your work.

A 5^2

B 3^2

C 3^5

D 5^3

Name_____

☐ **Ava bought 6 kg of honey. She divided it in 5 equal jars. Then she divided each jar of honey in 5 equal containers and so on. She repeated this process 4 times. How many equal amounts of honey did she get? Be sure to show your work.**

    A 4^5

    B 5^4

    C 4^6

    D 6^4

☐ **Write the expression below as a product.**

$$2^6$$

    A   2 x 2

    B   6 x 6

    C   2 x 2 x 2 x 2 x 2 x 2

    D   6 x 6 x 6 x 6 x 6 x 6

☐ **Tyler halved a pizza. Then he halved each piece of pizza and so on. He repeated this process 3 times. How many pieces of pizza did he get? Be sure to show your work.**

    A 2^2

    B 3^3

    C 2^3

    D 3^2

Name_____

Common Core Standard 6.EE.A.1 – Expressions & Equations

☐ Samantha investigates reproduction of amoeba. How many amoebae appear after 8 binary fissions? Be sure to show your work.

A 8^8

B 8^2

C 2^8

D 2^2

Common Core Standard 6.EE.A.1 – Expressions & Equations

☐ Solve for x below to find the correct answer. Be sure to show your work.

$$2^4 = x$$

A 6

B 8

C 16

D 24

Common Core Standard 6.EE.A.1 – Expressions & Equations

☐ Munya saves for a laptop. He put $2 in the bank in the 1st week. Then he doubled his deposit each week. How much money did Munya put in the bank in the 6th week? Be sure to show your work.

A 2^2

B 2^6

C 6^2

D 6^6

Common Core Standard 6.EE.A.1 – Expressions & Equations

☐ The chairs in the classroom are arranged in 5 rows and 5 columns. What is the number of chairs in the classroom? Be sure to show your work.

A 2^2

B 2^5

C 5^2

D 5^5

Common Core Standard 6.EE.A.1 – Expressions & Equations

☐ Write the following expression as an exponent.

$$3 \times 3 \times 3 \times 3 \times 3$$

A 3^5

B 5^3

C 3^3

D 5^5

Common Core Standard 6.EE.A.1 – Expressions & Equations

☐ There are 4 buildings on a street. Each building has 4 floors with 4 apartments on each floor. How many apartments are there on that street? Be sure to show your work.

A 3^3

B 4^3

C 3^4

D 4^4

Common Core Standard 6.EE.A.1 – Expressions & Equations

☐   How many small cubes are there in Rubik's cube? Be sure to show your work.

A 3^1

B 3^2

C 3^3

D 3^4

Common Core Standard 6.EE.A.1 – Expressions & Equations

☐   Evaluate the expression. Be sure to show your work.

$$\left(\frac{1}{2}\right)^3$$

A   1/5

B   1/6

C   1/8

D   1/9

Common Core Standard 6.EE.A.1 – Expressions & Equations

☐   The apple trees in the orchard are arranged in 8 rows and 8 columns. How many apple trees are there in the orchard? Be sure to show your work.

A 8^8

B 8^2

C 2^8

D 2^2

Name_____

Common Core Standard 6.EE.A.1 – Expressions & Equations

☐ **Benjamin bought 2 packs of juice with 2 bottle in each pack. Each juice bottle contains 2 l of juice. How many liters of juice did Benjamin buy? Be sure to show your work.**

A 2^2

B 2^3

C 3^2

D 3^3

Common Core Standard 6.EE.A.1 – Expressions & Equations

☐ **Write the following expression as a product.**

$$3^2$$

A 3 x 2

B 2 x 3

C 3 x 3

D 2 x 2 x 2

Common Core Standard 6.EE.A.1 – Expressions & Equations

☐ **Each of 4 girls has a bouquet of flowers with 4 flowers in a bouquet. Each flower has 4 petals. How many petals are there in all? Be sure to show your work.**

A 4^3

B 4^4

C 3^3

D 3^4

Common Core Standard 6.EE.A.1 – Expressions & Equations

☐ **How many apples are there in the bottom row in the picture below? Be sure to show your work.**

A 4^2

B 2^3

C 3^2

D 2^4

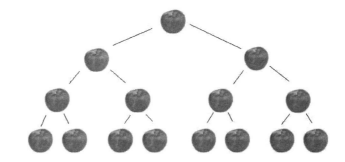

Common Core Standard 6.EE.A.1 – Expressions & Equations

☐ **Solve for x. Be sure to show your work.**

$$0.2^3 = x$$

A   8

B   0.8

C   0.08

D   0.008

Common Core Standard 6.EE.A.1 – Expressions & Equations

☐ **How many ants are there in the bottom row in the picture below? Be sure to show your work.**

A 3^2

B 3^3

C 2^2

D 2^3

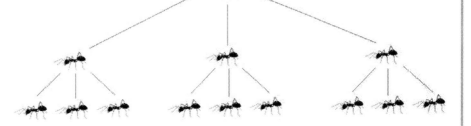

Common Core Standard 6.EE.A.2.A – The Number System

☐   There were x passengers in the bus. 12 of them left the bus on 1ˢᵗ station. How many passengers are left in the bus? Be sure to show your work.

A   12 - x

B   x - 12

C   x + 12

D   12x

Common Core Standard 6.EE.A.2.A – The Number System

☐   Write the expression for the sentence below.

"Subtract 7 from z"

A   z - 7

B   7 - z

C   -7 - z

D   - (z – 7)

Common Core Standard 6.EE.A.2.A – The Number System

☐   There were 6 strawberries in a plate. Marry added y strawberries. How many strawberries are there in a plate? Be sure to show your work.

A   6 - y

B   y – 6

C   6 + y

D   6y

Common Core Standard 6.EE.A.2.A – The Number System

☐ Andy has 2 boxes with *p* DVD's in each box. He added 3 DVD's in each box. How many DVD's are there in both boxes? Be sure to show your work.

A $3 (2 + p)$

B $p + 6$

C $2p + 3$

D $2 (p + 3)$

Common Core Standard 6.EE.A.2.A – The Number System

☐ Write the expression for the sentence below.

"Add 5 to x"

A $x + 5$

B $5x$

C $x - 5$

D $5 - x$

Common Core Standard 6.EE.A.2.A – The Number System

☐ Ray divided equally *t* plums in 3 bags. Then he ate 2 plums from the 1st bag. How many plums are left in the 1st bag? Be sure to show your work.

A $3t - 2$

B $\frac{t}{3} - 2$

C $3t + 2$

D $\frac{t}{3} + 2$

Common Core Standard 6.EE.A.2.A – The Number System

☐ Karen bought *k* six-pack of water. How many bottles of water did Karen buy? Be sure to show your work.

A   k + 6

B   k - 6

C   6 - k

D   6k

Common Core Standard 6.EE.A.2.A – The Number System

☐ Write the expression for the sentence below.

"Multiply t by 8"

A $\dfrac{t}{8}$

B   8t

C   t + 8

D   t - 8

Common Core Standard 6.EE.A.2.A – The Number System

☐ Lauren served *x* kg of ice cream in 5 cups. How much ice cream did Lauren out in each cup? Be sure to show your work.

A $\dfrac{x}{5}$

B $\dfrac{5}{x}$

C   5x

D   x + 5

Common Core Standard 6.EE.A.2.A – The Number System

☐ There were *y* plates with 6 apples in each plate. Rania took 2 apples from each plate. How many apples did Rania take? Be sure to show your work.

A   2 (y + 6)

B   6 (y + 2)

C   2y

D   6y

Common Core Standard 6.EE.A.2.A – The Number System

☐ Write the expression for the sentence below.

"Divide z by 4"

A $\dfrac{z}{4}$

B   4z

C $\dfrac{4}{z}$

D   z + 4

Common Core Standard 6.EE.A.2.A – The Number System

☐ Ryan cut a cake in *z* equal pieces. If a cake weighs 3 lb, how much does each piece weigh? Be sure to show your work.

A $\dfrac{z}{3}$

B $\dfrac{3}{z}$

C   3z

D   z - 3

Name_____

Common Core Standard 6.EE.A.2.A – The Number System

☐ There were *x* students in the art class at the beginning of the school year. Two months later 3 more students joined the class. How many students are there in the art class? Be sure to show your work.

A   x - 3

B   3 - x

C   x + 3

D   -x - 3

Common Core Standard 6.EE.A.2.A – The Number System

☐ Write the following calculation as an expression.

"Subtract x from 24"

A   x - 24

B   24 - x

C   x + 24

D   -x - 24

Common Core Standard 6.EE.A.2.A – The Number System

☐ There were 25 guests at Amelie's birthday party. After 9 P.M. *y* of them went home. How many guests stayed at the party after 9 P.M.? Be sure to show your work.

A   25 - y

B   y - 25

C   -y - 25

D   - (25 – y)

Name_____

Common Core Standard 6.EE.A.2.A – The Number System

☐   There are *z* rooms in the hotel with 4 guests in each room. One guest from each room went on a bus tour. How many guests are left in the hotel? Be sure to show your work.

A   4z

B   4z - 1

C   3z

D   z - 4

Common Core Standard 6.EE.A.2.A – The Number System

☐   Write the following calculation as an expression

"Add y to -6"

A   -6 + y

B   y + 6

C   -y + 6

D   -6y

Common Core Standard 6.EE.A.2.A – The Number System

☐   There are *t* cabbage heads in the garden arranged in 6 rows with equal number of cabbage heads in each row. Gary planted 2 more cabbage heads in the 3rd row. How many cabbage heads are there in the 3rd row? Be sure to show your work.

A   6t + 2

B $\frac{t}{6}$ + 2

C   6t - 2

D $\frac{t}{6}$ - 2

Common Core Standard 6.EE.A.2.A – The Number System

☐ **Jillian's Cakery has *x* racks with 12 cakes on each rack. How many cakes are there on all racks?**

A $\dfrac{x}{12}$

B $\dfrac{12}{x}$

C 12x

D 12 - x

Common Core Standard 6.EE.A.2.A – The Number System

☐ **Write the following calculation as an expression.**

"Multiply k by -2"

A k - 2

B -2k

C 2 - k

D 2k

Common Core Standard 6.EE.A.2.A – The Number System

☐ **There were *y* players at the tournament divided in 8 teams. How many players were on each team? Be sure to show your work.**

A $\dfrac{y}{8}$

B $\dfrac{8}{y}$

C 8y

D y - 8

Common Core Standard 6.EE.A.2.A – The Number System

☐   Each of *k* buses has 50 seats. 4 seats in each bus are reserved for passengers with monthly bus passes. How many seats in all buses are reserved for passengers with monthly bus passes? Be sure to show your work.

A   4 (k + 50)

B   50K + 4

C   4K + 50

D   4k

Common Core Standard 6.EE.A.2.A – The Number System

☐   Write the following calculation as an expression.

"Divide -8 by t"

A $\frac{8}{-t}$

B $\frac{t}{-8}$

C   -8t

D   t - 8

Common Core Standard 6.EE.A.2.A – The Number System

☐   120 soldiers are divided in *t* equal sized squads. How many soldiers are in each squad? Be sure to show your work.

A $\frac{120}{t}$

B $\frac{t}{120}$

C   120t

D   120 + t

Common Core Standard 6.EE.A.2.B – Expressions & Equations

Ralph spent *x* dollars in the restaurant and 20 dollars in the pet shop. The expression *x + 20* shows the total amount he spent. Which of the following is the term in the expression *x + 20*?

A   x

B   +

C   2

D   0

Common Core Standard 6.EE.A.2.B – Expressions & Equations

Identify the sum in the expression below.

$$4 (x + 2)$$

A   4

B   x + 2

C   x

D   2

Common Core Standard 6.EE.A.2.B – Expressions & Equations

There are 5 plates with *k* peaches in each plate. Farruk added 2 peaches on one plate. The expression *5k + 2* shows the total number of peaches. Which of the following is the coefficient in the expression *5k + 2*?

A   5k

B   2

C   5

D   5k + 2

Common Core Standard 6.EE.A.2.B – Expressions & Equations

The seats are arranged in 20 rows with x seats in each row. After removing 2 seats from each row the total number of seats is $20(x-2)$. Which of the following is the product in the expression $20(x-2)$?

A   20

B   x

C   x - 2

D   20 (x – 2)

Common Core Standard 6.EE.A.2.B – Expressions & Equations

Identify the factor in the expression below.

$$(x + 1) (y - 2)$$

A   x

B   y

C   x + 1

D   (x + 1) (y – 2)

Common Core Standard 6.EE.A.2.B – Expressions & Equations

3 friends divided equally x lb of ice cream. Each of them got $\frac{x}{3}$ lb of ice cream. Which of the following is the quotient in the expression $\frac{x}{3}$?

A   x

B   /

C   3

D $\frac{x}{3}$

Name_____

Common Core Standard 6.EE.A.2.B – Expressions & Equations

☐ The area of the floor is represented by the expression $(2x - 3)(y + 4)$. Which of the following is the sum in the expression $(2x - 3)(y + 4)$?

A $2x - 3$

B $y + 4$

C $2x$

D y

Common Core Standard 6.EE.A.2.B – Expressions & Equations

☐ The expression below is _____

$$c$$

A   Factor

B   Sum

C   Quotient

D   Term

Common Core Standard 6.EE.A.2.B – Expressions & Equations

☐ There are k students in each of 6 classrooms. The expression $6k$ shows the total number of students. Which of the following is the coefficient in the expression $6k$?

A   6

B k

C $6k$

D   None of the above

Common Core Standard 6.EE.A.2.B – Expressions & Equations

☐ There are 3 boxes with *x* toys in each box. Paul added 4 toys to each of the 3 boxes. The expression *3 (x + 4)* represents the total number of toys. Which of the following is the product in the expression *3 (x + 4)*?

A   3

B   4

C   x + 4

D   3 (x + 4)

Common Core Standard 6.EE.A.2.B – Expressions & Equations

☐ The expression below is _____

$$\frac{x - 3}{5}$$

A   Factor

B   Sum

C   Quotient

D   Term

Common Core Standard 6.EE.A.2.B – Expressions & Equations

☐ The number of rabbits in the forest is *5 (x + 3)*. Which of the following is the factor in the expression *5 (x + 3)*?

A   5

B   x

C   3

D   5 (x + 3)

Common Core Standard 6.EE.A.2.B – Expressions & Equations

☐ The number of legs of x cows and y chickens is represented by the expression *4x + 2y*. Which of the following is the sum in the expression *4x + 2y*?

A   4

B   4x

C   2y

D   4x + 2y

Common Core Standard 6.EE.A.2.B – Expressions & Equations

☐ Identify the coefficient in the expression below.

4x

A   4

B   x

C   4x

D   None of the above

Common Core Standard 6.EE.A.2.B – Expressions & Equations

☐ There are k cars on the parking lot. Which of the following is the expression k?

A   Coefficient

B   Product

C   Quotient

D   Term

Name_____

Common Core Standard 6.EE.A.2.B – Expressions & Equations

☐ The dimensions of the football pitch are *w* and *l*. The dimensions of the soccer field are *w - 10* and *l - 20*. The expression $(w - 10)(l - 20)$ represents the area of the soccer field. Which of the following is the factor in the expression $(w - 10)(l - 20)$?

A   w

B   l

C   w - 10

D $(w - 10)(l - 20)$

Common Core Standard 6.EE.A.2.B – Expressions & Equations

☐ Identify the product in the expression below.

$$6(3 - x)$$

A   6

B   x

C   3 - x

D $6(3 - x)$

Common Core Standard 6.EE.A.2.B – Expressions & Equations

☐ *K* notebooks are stored in 5 drawers, so that each drawer contains $\frac{k}{5}$ notebooks. The expression $\frac{k}{5}$ - 3 represents the number of notebooks in the drawer from which 3 notebooks are taken. Which of the following is the quotient in the expression $\frac{k}{5}$ - 3?

A   k

B   5

C $\frac{k}{5}$

D   3

Name_____

Common Core Standard 6.EE.A.2.B – Expressions & Equations

☐　　The basketball team has 6 players. Which of the following is 6?

　A　　Coefficient

　B　　Product

　C　　Factor

　D　　Term

Common Core Standard 6.EE.A.2.B – Expressions & Equations

☐　　Identify the sum in the expression below.

$$\frac{x - 3}{y + 6}$$

　A　　$x - 3$

　B　　$y + 6$

　C　　y

　D　　$\dfrac{x - 3}{y + 6}$

Common Core Standard 6.EE.A.2.B – Expressions & Equations

☐　　There are 2 bags with *k* cherries in each bag. The expression *2k* represents the total number of cherries. Which of the following is the coefficient in the expression *2k*?

　A　　2

　B　　k

　C　　2k

　D　　None of the above

Common Core Standard 6.EE.A.2.B – Expressions & Equations

There are 4 6-grade classes with x students in each class. Two weeks later 2 students are added to each of the 4 classes. The expression $4(x + 2)$ represents the total number of students in the 6th grade. Which of the following is the product in the expression $4(x + 2)$?

A x

B   2

C $x + 2$

D $4(x + 2)$

Common Core Standard 6.EE.A.2.B – Expressions & Equations

Identify the factor in the expression below.

$$(3x - 2) 6$$

A $3x$

B   2

C   6

D $(3x - 2) 6$

Common Core Standard 6.EE.A.2.B – Expressions & Equations

120 eggs are packed in t equal sized packs. 2 eggs are taken from one pack. The number of eggs in that pack is $\frac{120}{t} - 2$. Which of the following is the quotient in the expression $\frac{120}{t} - 2$?

A $\frac{120}{t}$

B   120

C t

D   2

Common Core Standard 6.EE.A.2.C – Expressions & Equations

☐ The swimming pool is 50 m long, 25 m wide, and 3 m deep. How many m³ of water are there in the swimming pool if the formula for the volume of the swimming pool is $V = l \times w \times d$, where l is length, w is width and d is depth of the swimming pool? Be sure to show your work.

A   3,250 m³

B   3,500 m³

C   3,750 m³

D   4,000 m³

Common Core Standard 6.EE.A.2.C – Expressions & Equations

☐ Find the value of the expression below for x = 2.5. Be sure to show your work.

$$2x + 3$$

A   8

B   9

C   10

D   11

Common Core Standard 6.EE.A.2.C – Expressions & Equations

☐ What is the perimeter of the rectangular playground the width w of which is 16 yd and the length l is 20 yd? Use formula for the perimeter of rectangle $P = 2 (w + l)$. Be sure to show your work.

A   36 yd

B   52 yd

C   56 yd

D   72 yd

Common Core Standard 6.EE.A.2.C – Expressions & Equations

☐ The cars on the dealership lot are arranged in *r* rows with *c* cars in each row. How many cars are there on the dealership lot if *r* = 6 and *c* = 8? Use formula *T* = *r* x *c*, where *T* is the total number of cars. Be sure to show your work.

A   14

B   48

C   68

D   86

Common Core Standard 6.EE.A.2.C – Expressions & Equations

☐ Find the value of the expression below for $x = \frac{1}{3}$. Be sure to show your work.

$$6 (x - 0.5)$$

A   -1

B   0

C   1

D   2

Common Core Standard 6.EE.A.2.C – Expressions & Equations

☐ The number of birds on the tree is represented by the expression *4t - 3*, where *t* is the temperature of the air. How many birds are there on the tree when the temperature is 22° *C*? Be sure to show your work.

A   76

B   79

C   82

D   85

Name_____

Common Core Standard 6.EE.A.2.C – Expressions & Equations

☐ What is the area of a cube shaped box the edge of which is 3 ft long? Use formula for the area of the cube $A = 6a^2$, where A is the area and a is the edge of the box. Be sure to show your work.

A   18 ft²

B   36 ft²

C   54 ft²

D   72 ft²

Common Core Standard 6.EE.A.2.C – Expressions & Equations

☐ Find the value of the expression below for $x = -2$ and $y = -5$. Be sure to show your work.

$$(2x - 3)(y + 1)$$

A   -28

B   -14

C   14

D   28

Common Core Standard 6.EE.A.2.C – Expressions & Equations

☐ The expression $100 - 2k$ represents the number of DVD players left in the store after k days. How many DVD players are left in the store after 10 days? Be sure to show your work.

A   980

B   98

C   90

D   80

Name_____

Common Core Standard 6.EE.A.2.C – Expressions & Equations

☐ What is the area of the matchbox that has a shape of a rectangular prism with the following dimensions: $w = 2$ cm, $l = 4$ cm, $h = 1$ cm? Use formula for the area of the matchbox $A = 2 (wl + lh + wh)$. Be sure to show your work.

A   8 cm²

B   14 cm²

C   16 cm²

D   28 cm²

Common Core Standard 6.EE.A.2.C – Expressions & Equations

☐ Find the value of the expression below using the rule for the order of operations. Be sure to show your work.

$$5 \times 2 - \frac{6}{2}$$

A   -10

B   -5

C   2

D   7

Common Core Standard 6.EE.A.2.C – Expressions & Equations

☐ What is the volume of Rubik's Cube the edge of which is 2 in. Use formula for the volume of the cube $V = a^3$, where V is a volume and a is the edge. Be sure to show your work.

A   5

B   6

C   8

D   23

Common Core Standard 6.EE.A.2.C – Expressions & Equations

☐ The expression *4x + 2y* represents the number of legs of *x* dogs and *y* birds. How many legs do 8 dogs and 12 birds have? Be sure to show your work.

A   20

B   40

C   56

D   64

Common Core Standard 6.EE.A.2.C – Expressions & Equations

☐ Find the value of the expression below using the rule for the order of operations. Be sure to show your work.

$$20/10 - 5 \times 2 + 4$$

A   -4

B   4

C   5

D   12

Common Core Standard 6.EE.A.2.C – Expressions & Equations

☐ The expression *4c + 2b* represents the number of wheels of *c* cars and *b* bicycles. How many wheels do 7 cars and 5 bicycles have? Be sure to show your work.

A   24

B   34

C   38

D   48

Name_____

Common Core Standard 6.EE.A.2.C – Expressions & Equations

☐   What is the area of the tennis court where the width *w* is 36 ft and length *l* is 78 ft? Use formula for the area of rectangle $A = w \times l$. Be sure to show your work.

A   2,408 ft^2

B   2,808 ft^2

C   3,208 ft^2

D   3,608 ft^2

Common Core Standard 6.EE.A.2.C – Expressions & Equations

☐   Find the value of the expression below using the rule for the order of operations. Be sure to show your work.

$$40 - 8/2 + 4 \times 2$$

A   24

B   40

C   44

D   80

Common Core Standard 6.EE.A.2.C – Expressions & Equations

☐   What is the perimeter of a square shaped tile with a side length *a* = 4 in? Use formula for the perimeter of a square $P = 4a$. Be sure to show your work.

A   4 in

B   8 in

C   16 in

D   44 in

Name_____

Common Core Standard 6.EE.A.2.C – Expressions & Equations

☐ The expression *4x + 6y* represents the number of bottles in *x* four-packs and *y* six-packs. How many bottles are there in 5 four-packs and 8 six-packs? Be sure to show your work.

A 52

B 62

C 68

D 78

Common Core Standard 6.EE.A.2.C – Expressions & Equations

☐ Find the value of the expression below for *x* = 2 and *y* = 4. Be sure to show your work.

$$5^x - y^2 + 2(x + y)$$

A -2

B 21

C 14

D 37

Common Core Standard 6.EE.A.2.C – Expressions & Equations

☐ The expression *f* x *b* represents the number of brochures in *b* tourist handouts with *f* brochures in each handout. How many brochures are there in 5 tourist handouts if each handout consists of 6 brochures? Be sure to show your work.

A 11

B 30

C 56

D 65

Name_____

Common Core Standard 6.EE.A.2.C – Expressions & Equations

☐ The expression *8s + 6b* represents the number of legs of *s* spiders and *b* butterflies. How many legs do 9 spiders and 5 butterflies have? Be sure to show your work.

A   84

B   94

C   102

D   112

Common Core Standard 6.EE.A.2.C – Expressions & Equations

☐ Find the value of the expression below for *x = -3* and *y = -2*. Be sure to show your work.

$$x^3 - \left(\frac{1}{2}\right)^y + xy$$

A   -25

B   -17

C   29

D   37

Common Core Standard 6.EE.A.2.C – Expressions & Equations

☐ The width *w* of a picture is 6 ft and the height *h* is 4 ft. What is the area of the picture? Use formula for the area of the rectangle *A = w x h*. Be sure to show your work.

A   10 ft^2

B   24 ft^2

C   46 ft^2

D   64 ft^2

Common Core Standard 6.EE.A.3 – Expressions & Equations

☐ The students are going on a field trip in 3 buses. There are *k* students and 2 drivers in each bus. The total number of people in 3 buses is *3 (k + 2)*. Which expression also represents the total number of people in 3 buses? Be sure to show your work.

A   3k + 2

B   3k + 5

C   3k + 6

D   3k + 32

Common Core Standard 6.EE.A.3 – Expressions & Equations

☐ Which expression is equivalent to the expression below?

$$x + x + x + x$$

A x^4

B 4^x

C   xxxx

D   4x

Common Core Standard 6.EE.A.3 – Expressions & Equations

☐ Miriam had *x* mellons in each of 4 boxes. After she added 2 mellons to one box the total number of mellons was *4x + 2*. Which expression also represents the total number of mellons? Be sure to show your work.

A   2(2x + 1)

B   4 (x + 2)

C   2 (2x + 2)

D   4 (x + 1)

Name_____

Common Core Standard 6.EE.A.3 – Expressions & Equations

☐   Hannah put 2 parots in each of *y* cages. The total number of parots is *2y*. Which expression also represents the total number of parots?   Be sure to show your work.

A $y + y$

B y^2

C 2^y

D $2 + 2$

Common Core Standard 6.EE.A.3 – Expressions & Equations

☐   Which expression is equivalent to the expression below? Be sure to show your work.

$$3 (4 - 2x)$$

A $12 - 6x$

B $7 - 5x$

C $7 - x$

D $12 - 2x$

Common Core Standard 6.EE.A.3 – Expressions & Equations

☐   Brady has a pet store. He has 4 aquariums with *x* fish in each aquarium. After he sold 12 fish, the total number of fish is *4x – 12*. Which expression also represents the total number of fish in the pet store? Be sure to show your work.

A $4 (x - 12)$

B $4 (x - 3)$

C $3 (x - 4)$

D $3 (x - 12)$

Name_____

Common Core Standard 6.EE.A.3 – Expressions & Equations

☐ There are *m* chocolate covered plums in each of 5 chocolate boxes. Jessica ate 2 chocolate covered plums from each box. The total number of chocolate covered plums left in the boxes is *5 (m – 2)*. Which expression also represents the total number of chocolate covered plums left in the boxes? Be sure to show your work.

A   5m – 2

B   m – 10

C   5m – 10

D   m – 7

Common Core Standard 6.EE.A.3 – Expressions & Equations

☐ Which expression is equivalent to the expression below? Be sure to show your work.

$$8x + 20$$

A   8 (x + 20)

B   8 (x + 2)

C   4 (2x + 10)

D   4 (2x + 5)

Common Core Standard 6.EE.A.3 – Expressions & Equations

☐ The expression *z + z + z* represents the number of chewing gums in 3 packs. Which expression also represents the number of chewing gums in 3 packs? Be sure to show your work.

A 3^z

B z^3

C   6z

D   3z

Common Core Standard 6.EE.A.3 – Expressions & Equations

☐ The perimeter of a receptions hall is *2 (w + l)*, where *w* is width and *l* is the length of the hall. Which expression also represents the perimeter of the receptions hall? Be sure to show your work.

A   *2w + 2l*

B   *2x + l*

C   *w + 2l*

D   *2wl*

Common Core Standard 6.EE.A.3 – Expressions & Equations

☐ Which expression is equivalent to the expression below? Be sure to show your work.

$$5t$$

A 5^t

B   5 + 5 + 5 + 5 + 5

C   t + t + t + t + t

D t^5

Common Core Standard 6.EE.A.3 – Expressions & Equations

☐ There were *k* birds on each of 6 trees. After 9 birds flew away, the number of birds left was *6k – 9*. Which expression also represents the number of birds left? Be sure to show your work.

A   6(k – 9)

B   2(k – 6)

C   6(k – 3)

D   3(2k – 3)

Name_____

☐ There are *n* passengers in each of 3 trains. The total number of passengers is *3n*. Which expression also represents the total number of passengers? Be sure to show your work.

A $n^3 + n^3 + n^3$

B $3n + 3n + 3n$

C $3 + 3 + 3$

D $n + n + n$

☐ Which expression is equivalent to the expression below? Be sure to show your work.

$$6\left(\frac{1}{3}x - 0.5\right)$$

A $2x - 3$

B $2x - 0.5$

C $\frac{1}{3}x - 3$

D $\frac{1}{3}x - 0.3$

☐ The expression *4c + 2b* represents the number of wheels of *c* cars and *b* bicycles. Which expression also represents the total number of wheels? Be sure to show your work.

A $4(c + 2b)$

B $2(2c + b)$

C $4(c + b)$

D $2(2c + 2b)$

Common Core Standard 6.EE.A.3 – Expressions & Equations

The width *w* of the playground is increased by 2 yd, and the length is 12 yd. The area of the playground is *12 (w + 2)*. Which expression also represents the area of the playground? Be sure to show your work.

A   12w + 2

B   12w + 24

C   12w + 14

D   12w + 122

Common Core Standard 6.EE.A.3 – Expressions & Equations

Which expression is equivalent to the expression below? Be sure to show your work.

2y + 2y + 2y + 2y

A   16y

B   8y

C   4y

D   2y

Common Core Standard 6.EE.A.3 – Expressions & Equations

The seats in the theater were arranged in 22 rows with *k* seats in each row. After removing 11 seats, the total number of seats was *22k – 11*. Which expression also represents the total number of seats? Be sure to show your work.

A   11(11K – 1)

B   11 (2k – 1)

C   22 (k – 1)

D   22 (k – 11)

Common Core Standard 6.EE.A.3 – Expressions & Equations

☐ There were 7 centerpieces with *m* acorns in each centerpiece. After Maddison removed 1 acorn from each centerpiece, the total number of acorns was *7 (m – 1)*. Which expression also represents the total number of acorns? Be sure to show your work.

A   7m – 7

B   7m – 1

C   7m – 8

D   7m – 6

Common Core Standard 6.EE.A.3 – Expressions & Equations

☐ Which expression is equivalent to the expression below? Be sure to show your work.

$$2 (3x + 0.5)$$

A   5x + 2.5

B   23x + 20.5

C   6x + 0.5

D   6x + 1

Common Core Standard 6.EE.A.3 – Expressions & Equations

☐ The expression *2x + 2x + 2x* represents the number of marbles in 3 bags. Which expression also represents the total number of marbles? Be sure to show your work.

A   3x

B   4x

C   5x

D   6x

Common Core Standard 6.EE.A.3 – Expressions & Equations

The expression *4x + 2y* represents the number of books read *x* by Niseem and *y* by Gagham. Which expression also represents the total number of books read? Be sure to show your work.

A   4 (x + 2y)

B   2 (4x + y)

C   4 (x + y)

D   2 (2x + y)

Common Core Standard 6.EE.A.3 – Expressions & Equations

Which expression is equivalent to the expression below? Be sure to show your work.

3k + 2k

A   k + k

B   2 + 2 + 3 + 3 + 3

C   3 + 3 + 2 + 2 +2

D   k + k + k + k + k

Common Core Standard 6.EE.A.3 – Expressions & Equations

Daniel had *t* books on each of 4 shelves. After he took 3 books from each shelf the total number of books was *4 (t – 3)*. Which expression also represents the total number of books left? Be sure to show your work.

A   4t – 3

B   4t – 12

C   4t – 1

D   4t – 7

Common Core Standard 6.EE.A.4 – Expressions & Equations

☐ The expression *x* + *x* + *x* + *x* represents the number of pears in 4 bags. Which expression is equivalent to the expression above? Be sure to show your work.

A   4 (x + 1)

B   4 (x + 4)

C   4x + 1

D   4x

Common Core Standard 6.EE.A.4 – Expressions & Equations

☐ Which expression is equivalent to the expression below? Be sure to show your work.

3(2t)

A   32t

B   6t

C   5t

D   t

Common Core Standard 6.EE.A.4 – Expressions & Equations

☐ Carol spent 6*t* dollars to buy *t* shirts priced at $6 each. Which expression also shows the amount of money Carol spent? Be sure to show your work.

A   t + t + t + t + t + t

B   6 + 6 + 6 + 6 + 6 + 6

C   6 + t + 6 + t + 6 + t

D   6 + t

Common Core Standard 6.EE.A.4 – Expressions & Equations

☐ The expression *5(p – 1)* represents the number of crystals on 5 lamps. Which expression is equivalent to the expression above? Be sure to show your work.

A   5p – 6

B   5p – 5

C   5p – 4

D   5p – 1

Common Core Standard 6.EE.A.4 – Expressions & Equations

☐ Which expression is equivalent to the expression below? Be sure to show your work.

$$y + y + y$$

A   3y + 1

B   3(y + 3)

C   3y + 3

D   3y

Common Core Standard 6.EE.A.4 – Expressions & Equations

☐ Austine sold *3k + 12* pumpkins in *k* hours. Which expression also shows the number of pumpkins Austine sold? Be sure to show your work.

A   3(k + 12)

B   4(k + 3)

C   3(k + 4)

D   4(k + 12)

Common Core Standard 6.EE.A.4 – Expressions & Equations

☐ The expression *2x + 2x + 2x* represents the number of lions in 3 state zoos. Which expression is equivalent to the expression above? Be sure to show your work.

A   2x

B   3x

C   5x

D   6x

Common Core Standard 6.EE.A.4 – Expressions & Equations

☐ Which expression is equivalent to the expression below? Be sure to show your work.

$$3(5 - z)$$

A   8 – 3z

B   8 – z

C   15 – 3z

D   15 – z

Common Core Standard 6.EE.A.4 – Expressions & Equations

☐ There are *4n* potato vines arranged in 4 rows in Lucy's garden. Which expression also shows the number of potato vines in Lucy's garden? Be sure to show your work.

A   n + n + n + n

B   4 + 4 + 4 + 4

C   4n + 4

D   44n

Common Core Standard 6.EE.A.4 – Expressions & Equations

☐ The expression *4(s + 1)* represents the number of participants during 4 local charity events. Which expression is equivalent to the expression above? Be sure to show your work.

A   4s + 4

B   4s + 1

C   4s + 5

D   4s + 41

Common Core Standard 6.EE.A.4 – Expressions & Equations

☐ Which expression is equivalent to the expression below? Be sure to show your work.

$$20 - 4d$$

A   5(4 – d)

B   20(1 – 4d)

C   4(20 – d)

D   4(5 – d)

Common Core Standard 6.EE.A.4 – Expressions & Equations

☐ Anna ran *10t – 4* miles in *t* hours. Which expression also shows the distance that Anna ran in *t* hours? Be sure to show your work.

A   10(*t* – 4)

B   4(10t – 1)

C   2(5t – 2)

D   2(5t – 4)

Name_____

Common Core Standard 6.EE.A.4 – Expressions & Equations

☐ The expression *a + a + b + b + b* represents the number of red dresses in 5 department stores. Which expression is equivalent to the expression above? Be sure to show your work.

A   5ab

B   2a x 3b

C   2a + 3b

D   5(a + b)

Common Core Standard 6.EE.A.4 – Expressions & Equations

☐ Which expression is equivalent to the expression below? Be sure to show your work.

(5u)(2v)

A   7uv

B   10uv

C   25uv

D   52uv

Common Core Standard 6.EE.A.4 – Expressions & Equations

☐ Noah collected *3c + 4d* small and big collectible cars. Which expression also shows the number of cars that Noah has collected so far? Be sure to show your work.

A   c + c + c + d + d + d + d

B   c + c + c + c + d + d + d

C   3 + 3 + 3 + 4 + 4 + 4 + 4

D   3 + 3 + 3 + 3 + 4 + 4 + 4

Common Core Standard 6.EE.A.4 – Expressions & Equations

☐ The expression *2x(y – 4)* represents the salary of *x* employees who have *y* years of work experience. Which expression is equivalent to the expression above? Be sure to show your work.

A   8xy

B   2xy – 4

C   -8xy

D   2xy – 8x

Common Core Standard 6.EE.A.4 – Expressions & Equations

☐ Which expression is equivalent to the expression below? Be sure to show your work.

$$3m + 3m + 3m + 3m$$

A   3 (m + 4)

B   3(4m + 1)

C   12m

D $12m^4$

Common Core Standard 6.EE.A.4 – Expressions & Equations

☐ Brianna bought *6x + 9y* drawing pencils and framing mats. Which expression also shows the number of pencils and mats that Brianna bought? Be sure to show your work.

A   3(2x + 3y)

B   3(3x + 6y)

C   6(x + 3y)

D   6(x + 9y)

Common Core Standard 6.EE.A.4 – Expressions & Equations

☐ The expression *ab* + *ab* + *bc* + *bc* + *ac* + *ac* represents the area of a rectangular prism. Which expression is equivalent to the expression above? Be sure to show your work.

A   2abc

B   2a(b+ c)

C   2(a + b + c)

D   2(ab + bc + ac)

Common Core Standard 6.EE.A.4 – Expressions & Equations

☐ Which expression is equivalent to the expression below? Be sure to show your work.

$$(m - 2)4n$$

A   4mn – 2n

B   4mn – 6n

C   4mn – 8n

D   4mn + 2n

Common Core Standard 6.EE.A.4 – Expressions & Equations

☐ The area of 5 rectangular playgrounds is *5ab*. Which expression also shows the area of 5 rectangular playgrounds? Be sure to show your work.

A   5 + a + b

B   ab + ab + ab + ab + ab

C   5 + 5 + 5 + 5 + 5

D   5 + ab

Name_____

Common Core Standard 6.EE.A.4 – Expressions & Equations

☐ The expression *a*(2*b* – 5) represents the number of chairs in *a* rows and *b* columns. Which expression is equivalent to the expression above? Be sure to show your work.

    A   2ab – 10

    B   2ab – 5

    C   2ab – 5a

    D   2ab – 10a

Common Core Standard 6.EE.A.4 – Expressions & Equations

☐ Which expression is equivalent to the expression below? Be sure to show your work.

15ab - 25b

    A   15b(a – 10)

    B   15b(a – 25)

    C   5b(3a – 25)

    D   5b(3a – 5)

Common Core Standard 6.EE.A.4 – Expressions & Equations

☐ David read *21d + 14* pages of his favorite book in *d* days. Which expression also shows the number of pages David read? Be sure to show your work.

    A   7(3d + 2)

    B   7(3d + 7)

    C   14(7d + 1)

    D   14(7d + 14)

Common Core Standard 6.EE.B.5 – Expressions & Equations

☐ **Matthew had 12 shirts. After he bought *x* shirts he had 21 shirts. Which number is the solution of the corresponding equation *12 + x = 21*? Be sure to show your work.**

A   -33

B   -9

C   9

D   33

Common Core Standard 6.EE.B.5 – Expressions & Equations

☐ **Solve for *t* in the expression below. Be sure to show your work.**

$$4 - t = 13$$

A   -17

B   -9

C   9

D   17

Common Core Standard 6.EE.B.5 – Expressions & Equations

☐ **Grace had *c* toys. She gave 6 toys to Marnie and was left with 8 toys. Which number is the solution of the corresponding equation *c – 6 = 8* ? Be sure to show your work.**

A   -14

B   -2

C   2

D   14

Common Core Standard 6.EE.B.5 – Expressions & Equations

☐   There are *y* snack packs in each of 5 isles, and 3 snack packs in the 6th isle for a total number of 28 snack packs in the C-Store. Which number is the solution of the corresponding equation *5y + 3 = 28*? Be sure to show your work.

    A   4

    B   5

    C   6

    D   7

Common Core Standard 6.EE.B.5 – Expressions & Equations

☐   Solve for *m* in the expression below. Be sure to show your work.

$$m - 7 = -3$$

    A   -10

    B   -4

    C   4

    D   10

Common Core Standard 6.EE.B.5 – Expressions & Equations

☐   Hannah had 27 watermelons. She sold *k* watermelons and is left with 11 watermelons. Which number is the solution of the corresponding equation *27 – k = 11*? Be sure to show your work.

    A   -38

    B   -16

    C   16

    D   38

Common Core Standard 6.EE.B.5 – Expressions & Equations

☐ Samuel arranged 33 marbles in 6 rows with z marbles in each row. He put in the 7th row the remaining 3 marbles. Which number is the solution of the corresponding equation $33 = 6z + 3$? Be sure to show your work.

A   6

B   5

C   -5

D   -6

Common Core Standard 6.EE.B.5 – Expressions & Equations

☐ Solve for n in the expression below. Be sure to show your work.

$$-8 + n = -2$$

A   -10

B   -6

C   6

D   10

Common Core Standard 6.EE.B.5 – Expressions & Equations

☐ The temperature in the morning was -3°C. The temperature increased for x°C to 4°C in the afternoon. Which number is the solution of the corresponding equation $-3 + x = 4$? Be sure to show your work.

A   7

B   1

C   -1

D   -7

Name_____

Common Core Standard 6.EE.B.5 – Expressions & Equations

☐ There were 4 plates with *p* cookies in each plate. Joshua added 3 cookies in each plate for the total number of 28 cookies. Which number is the solution of the corresponding equation *4(p + 3) = 28*? Be sure to show your work.

A   -10

B   -4

C   4

D   10

Common Core Standard 6.EE.B.5 – Expressions & Equations

☐ Solve for *q* in the expression below. Be sure to show your work.

$$-q - 12 = 7$$

A   -19

B   -5

C   5

D   19

Common Core Standard 6.EE.B.5 – Expressions & Equations

☐ There were *x* visitors at the art exhibition. Additional 7 visitors came, and the number of visitors became 43. Which number is the solution of the corresponding equation *x + 7 = 43*? Be sure to show your work.

A   -50

B   -36

C   36

D   50

Common Core Standard 6.EE.B.5 – Expressions & Equations

☐   The seats in the City Hall are arranged in 20 rows with *k* seats in each row. After removing 40 seats, the total number of seats is 160. Which number is the solution of the corresponding equation *20k – 40 = 160*? Be sure to show your work.

A   10

B   6

C   -6

D   -10

Common Core Standard 6.EE.B.5 – Expressions & Equations

☐   Solve for *b* in the expression below. Be sure to show your work.

$$16 - 2b = 6$$

A   -11

B   -5

C   5

D   11

Common Core Standard 6.EE.B.5 – Expressions & Equations

☐   Ella had *x* lb of sugar in the bag. After she added 1/2 lb of sugar the total weight of sugar became 2 lb Which number is the solution of the corresponding equation $x + \frac{1}{2} = 2$? Be sure to show your work.

A $-2\frac{1}{2}$

B $-1\frac{1}{2}$

C $1\frac{1}{2}$

D $2\frac{1}{2}$

Name_____

Common Core Standard 6.EE.B.5 – Expressions & Equations

☐   The pack of toothpicks contains *t* toothpicks. John took 4 toothpicks from each of 3 packs. The total number of toothpicks is now 138. Which number is the solution of the corresponding equation $3(t - 4) = 138$? Be sure to show your work.

A   -50

B   -42

C   42

D   50

Common Core Standard 6.EE.B.5 – Expressions & Equations

☐   Solve for *p* in the expression below. Be sure to show your work.

$$-4p - 8 = 20$$

A   -7

B   -3

C   3

D   7

Common Core Standard 6.EE.B.5 – Expressions & Equations

☐   There are *x* students in the class. 3/4 of them joined the group of 12 students from the other class who attend choir. The total number of students who attend choir is 48. Which number is the solution of the corresponding equation $\frac{3}{4}x + 12 = 48$? Be sure to show your work.

A   27

B   45

C   48

D   80

Common Core Standard 6.EE.B.5 – Expressions & Equations

☐ There were *k* students in 5 classes. 2 students from each class went on a math competition. The total number of students left is 115. Which number is the solution of the corresponding equation *5(k – 2) = 115*? Be sure to show your work.

A   21

B   23

C   25

D   27

Common Core Standard 6.EE.B.5 – Expressions & Equations

☐ Solve for *x* in the expression below. Be sure to show your work.

$$-7 + 2x = 13$$

A   -10

B   -3

C   3

D   10

Common Core Standard 6.EE.B.5 – Expressions & Equations

☐ Trinity had 12 lb of rice. She cooked *x* lb and now she has 7.50 lb. Which number is the solution of the corresponding equation *12 – x = 7.50*? Be sure to show your work.

A   5.50

B   4.50

C   -4.50

D   -5.50

Common Core Standard 6.EE.B.5 – Expressions & Equations

☐ **Samantha had 56 beeds. She used *v* beeds to make a bracelet for her friend and now she has 42 beeds. Which number is the solution of the corresponding equation *56 – v = 24*? Be sure to show your work.**

A   80

B   32

C   -32

D   -80

Common Core Standard 6.EE.B.5 – Expressions & Equations

☐ **Solve for *w* in the expression below. Be sure to show your work.**

$$8(2 - w) = -16$$

A   -4

B   -2

C   2

D   4

Common Core Standard 6.EE.B.5 – Expressions & Equations

☐ **Half of *z* employees in the company are women. 6 women left the company, and now the total number of women employees is 68. Which number is the solution of the corresponding equation $\frac{z}{2} - 6 = 68$? Be sure to show your work.**

A   31

B   37

C   124

D   148

Common Core Standard 6.EE.B.6 – Expressions & Equations

☐ **Ethan used 6 matches from the matchbox which contains _k_ matches. How many matches are left in the matchbox? Be sure to show your work.**

A   6k

B   6 – k

C   k – 6

D   k + 6

Common Core Standard 6.EE.B.6 – Expressions & Equations

☐ **Calculate for _m = 4_ in the expression below. Be sure to show your work.**

$$8 - 3m$$

A   -20

B   -4

C   4

D   20

Common Core Standard 6.EE.B.6 – Expressions & Equations

☐ **48 people are divided in 6 equal groups with _t_ people in each group. Which of the following expressions represents this scenario? Be sure to show your work.**

A   6t = 48

B   6t < 48

C   6t > 48

D   48 – 6t

Common Core Standard 6.EE.B.6 – Expressions & Equations

☐ The expression *5n* represents the number of fingers on *n* hands. How many fingers are there on 8 hands? Be sure to show your work.

A   5n + 8

B   5n – 8

C   13

D   40

Common Core Standard 6.EE.B.6 – Expressions & Equations

☐ Calculate for *x = -3* in the expression below. Be sure to show your work.

$$2x - 7$$

A   -13

B   -1

C   1

D   13

Common Core Standard 6.EE.B.6 – Expressions & Equations

☐ Benjamin added 8 badges to his collection of *y* badges. Now he has more than 90 badges. Which of the following expressions represents this scenario? Be sure to show your work.

A   90 + y > 8

B   8 + y > 90

C   90y > 8

D   8y > 90

Common Core Standard 6.EE.B.6 – Expressions & Equations

[ ] The price of a glass is $x and the price of a plate is $y. Roberta bought 8 glasses and 5 plates. Which of the following expressions represents the total amount of money she spent? Be sure to show your work.

A   8x + 5y

B   5x + 8y

C   8x – 5y

D   5x – 8y

Common Core Standard 6.EE.B.6 – Expressions & Equations

[ ] Calculate for *a = -2, b = 4* in the expression below. Be sure to show your work.

$$5b - 3a$$

A   -22

B   -2

C   14

D   26

Common Core Standard 6.EE.B.6 – Expressions & Equations

[ ] There were 100 people at the theater. After 3 groups of *t* people left the theater, 64 people were left in the theater. Which of the following expressions represents this scenario? Be sure to show your work.

A   3t – 64 = 100

B   100 – 3t = 64

C   64 – 3t = 100

D   3t – 100 = 64

Name_____

Common Core Standard 6.EE.B.6 – Expressions & Equations

☐ Taxi driver charges *5y + 3* dollars for *y* miles. How much does taxi driver charge for 4 miles? Be sure to show your work.

A $57

B $35

C $23

D $12

Common Core Standard 6.EE.B.6 – Expressions & Equations

☐ Calculate for *x = 3, y = -5* in the expression below. Be sure to show your work.

3x + 4y

A   -29

B   -11

C   11

D   29

Common Core Standard 6.EE.B.6 – Expressions & Equations

☐ There were *s* airplanes at the DFW airport. After 4 airplanes took off, the number of airplanes still parked was less than 8. Which of the following expressions represents this scenario? Be sure to show your work.

A $s - 4 < 8$

B $4 - s < 8$

C $s + 4 < 8$

D $s + 8 < 4$

Common Core Standard 6.EE.B.6 – Expressions & Equations

☐ There were 46 animals in the zoo. The manager of the zoo sold *x* animals. How many animals were left in the zoo? Be sure to show your work.

A $x - 46$

B $46 - x$

C $x + 46$

D $46x$

Common Core Standard 6.EE.B.6 – Expressions & Equations

☐ Which number is the solution of the equation below? Be sure to show your work.

$$x + 12 = 3$$

A   -15

B   -9

C   9

D   15

Common Core Standard 6.EE.B.6 – Expressions & Equations

☐ Olivia found 6 boxes with *t* books in each box in the basement. How many books did Olivia find in the basement? Be sure to show your work.

A $6t$

B $6 - t$

C $t - 6$

D $t + 6$

Name_____

Common Core Standard 6.EE.B.6 – Expressions & Equations

☐ The expression $\frac{120}{n}$ represents the number of eggs in each of *n* packs. How many eggs are there in a pack, if there are 10 packs? Be sure to show your work.

A   6

B   10

C   12

D   20

Common Core Standard 6.EE.B.6 – Expressions & Equations

☐ Which number is the solution of the inequallity below? Be sure to show your work.

$$6 - p < 2$$

A   -10

B   -5

C   3

D   10

Common Core Standard 6.EE.B.6 – Expressions & Equations

☐ 3 players were removed from the team of *k* players because they were disqualified. Now the number of players is less than 14. Which of the following expressions represents this scenario? Be sure to show your work.

A $k - 3 < 14$

B $3 - k < 14$

C $k + 14 < 3$

D $14 - k < 3$

Common Core Standard 6.EE.B.6 – Expressions & Equations

☐ The expression *2l + 2w* represents the perimeter of the doctor's office. If the width *w* is 4 ft and the length *l* is 5 ft, what is the perimeter of the office? Be sure to show your work.

A 9 ft

B 12 ft

C 15 ft

D 18 ft

Common Core Standard 6.EE.B.6 – Expressions & Equations

☐ Which set of numbers contains the solution of the equation below? Be sure to show your work.

$$2y - 6 = -2$$

A {1,3,5}

B {2,4,6}

C {-1,-3,-5}

D {-2,-4,-6}

Common Core Standard 6.EE.B.6 – Expressions & Equations

☐ Sophia has $154. She put money in 3 saving boxes, one for each upcoming occasion with $*k* in each box, and the remaining $4 Sophia put in her pocket. Which of the following expressions represents this scenario? Be sure to show your work.

A 3k + 4 = 154

B 4k + 3 = 154

C 3k – 4 = 154

D 4k – 3 = 154

Common Core Standard 6.EE.B.6 – Expressions & Equations

☐ The altitude of the elevator is represented by the expression *20 – 2t*, where *t* is the time in seconds. What is the altitude of the elevator after 4 seconds? Be sure to show your work.

A   40

B   28

C   12

D   0

Common Core Standard 6.EE.B.6 – Expressions & Equations

☐ Which set of numbers contains the solution of the inequality below? Be sure to show your work.

$$3 - p < -2$$

A   {-1,-3,-5}

B   {-2,-4,-6}

C   {1,3,5}

D   {2,4,6}

Common Core Standard 6.EE.B.6 – Expressions & Equations

☐ In the last 5 days Ray earned $*m*. Today he earned $20 and now he has more than $150. Which of the following expressions represents this scenario? Be sure to show your work.

A   5m + 20 > 150

B   5m – 20 > 150

C   5m + 150 > 20

D   5m – 150 > 20

Common Core Standard 6.EE.B.7 – Expressions & Equations

Amber had x friends. She acquanted with 4 girls at church and now she has 23 friends. Solve for *x* corresponding equation *x + 4 = 23*. Be sure to show your work.

A   19

B   27

C   21

D   25

Common Core Standard 6.EE.B.7 – Expressions & Equations

Solve for *x* in the expression below. Be sure to show your work.

$$x + \frac{1}{2} = 3$$

A $3\frac{1}{2}$

B   3

C $2\frac{1}{2}$

D   2

Common Core Standard 6.EE.B.7 – Expressions & Equations

There are *x* cards in each of 4 decks. The total number of cards is 128. Solve for *x* corresponding equation *4x = 128*. Be sure to show your work.

A   512

B   132

C   124

D   32

Common Core Standard 6.EE.B.7 – Expressions & Equations

☐ **Timothy has a collection of 84 baseball cards. He gave *x* cards to his brother and now he has 56 baseball cards. Solve for *x* corresponding equation *84 – x = 56*. Be sure to show your work.**

A   140

B   70

C   56

D   28

Common Core Standard 6.EE.B.7 – Expressions & Equations

☐ **Solve for *x* in the expression below. Be sure to show your work.**

$$\frac{1}{3}x = 6$$

A   2

B $5\frac{2}{3}$

C $6\frac{1}{3}$

D   18

Common Core Standard 6.EE.B.7 – Expressions & Equations

☐ **Sarah had 45 candles. For Hannukkah she made *t* candle arrangements with 9 candles in each. Solve for *x* corresponding equation *9x = 45*. Be sure to show your work.**

A   5

B   24

C   36

D   180

Common Core Standard 6.EE.B.7 – Expressions & Equations

☐ **Nitti has 3 1/2 kg and Raena has *x* kg of of coconut mix. Together they have 5 kg of the mix. Solve for *x* corresponding equation $3\frac{1}{2} + x = 5$. Be sure to show your work.**

A   16

B $15\frac{1}{2}$

C $8\frac{1}{2}$

D $1\frac{1}{2}$

Common Core Standard 6.EE.B.7 – Expressions & Equations

☐ **Solve for *x* in the expression below. Be sure to show your work.**

$$x - 2 = 1\frac{1}{3}$$

A $\frac{1}{3}$

B $1\frac{1}{2}$

C $2\frac{1}{3}$

D $3\frac{1}{3}$

Common Core Standard 6.EE.B.7 – Expressions & Equations

☐ **The total weight of 8 packs of rice with *t* kg of rice in each pack is 4 kg. Solve for *x* corresponding equation *8x = 4*. Be sure to show your work.**

A $\frac{1}{2}$

B   2

C   4

D   12

Common Core Standard 6.EE.B.7 – Expressions & Equations

☐ **Jasmine had $12.50. She spent $x in the grocery and left with $4. Solve for x corresponding equation 12.5 – x = 4. Be sure to show your work.**

A   3.125

B   8.5

C   16.5

D   50

Common Core Standard 6.EE.B.7 – Expressions & Equations

☐ **Solve for x in the expression below. Be sure to show your work.**

$$3\frac{1}{3} - x = 1\frac{2}{3}$$

A $1\frac{1}{3}$

B $1\frac{2}{3}$

C $2\frac{1}{3}$

D $2\frac{2}{3}$

Common Core Standard 6.EE.B.7 – Expressions & Equations

☐ **The length of a tile is 5 1/4 in. The length of x tiles is 31 1/2 in. Solve for x corresponding equation $5\frac{1}{4}x = 31\frac{1}{2}$. Be sure to show your work.**

A   5

B $5\frac{1}{2}$

C   6

D $6\frac{1}{2}$

Name_____

Common Core Standard 6.EE.B.7 – Expressions & Equations

☐ The Coconut Barfi weighs x kg. Ajun ate 0.25 kg of cake. The remaining cake weighs 2.5 kg. Solve for x corresponding equation $x – 0.25 = 2.5$. Be sure to show your work.

A   2.25

B   2.75

C   6.25

D   10

Common Core Standard 6.EE.B.7 – Expressions & Equations

☐ Solve for x in the expression below. Be sure to show your work.

$$x + 4.35 = 6.65$$

A   2.3

B   3

C   10.3

D   11

Common Core Standard 6.EE.B.7 – Expressions & Equations

☐ Justin scored 0.5 points on each of x tasks on the math test. His total score was 6.5 points. Solve for x corresponding equation $0.5x = 6.5$. Be sure to show your work.

A   5

B   7

C   13

D   14

Name_____

Common Core Standard 6.EE.B.7 – Expressions & Equations

☐ The height of grass was *x* in. The grass has grown 0.25 in and now its height is 6.75 in. Solve for *x* corresponding equation *x + 0.25 = 6.75*. Be sure to show your work.

A   5.5

B   6

C   6.5

D   7

Common Core Standard 6.EE.B.7 – Expressions & Equations

☐ Solve for *x* in the expression below. Be sure to show your work.

$$0.4x = 5$$

A   0.45

B   0.54

C   2

D   12.5

Common Core Standard 6.EE.B.7 – Expressions & Equations

☐ 3 kg of cream rolls is shared equaly among *x* friends, so that each of them gets 0.25 kg of cream rolls. Solve for *x* corresponding equation *0.25x = 3*. Be sure to show your work.

A   12

B   11

C   10

D   9

Common Core Standard 6.EE.B.7 – Expressions & Equations

☐   **Evelyn was selling 5 1/2 kg of Girl Scout cookies. She sold x kg to Blake and now she has 3 1/4 kg of cookies. Solve for x corresponding equation $5\frac{1}{2} - x = 3\frac{1}{4}$. Be sure to show your work.**

    A $2\frac{1}{2}$

    B $2\frac{1}{4}$

    C $1\frac{1}{2}$

    D $1\frac{1}{4}$

Common Core Standard 6.EE.B.7 – Expressions & Equations

☐   **Solve for x in the expression below. Be sure to show your work.**

$$x - 2.3 = 3$$

    A   5.3

    B   2.6

    C   2

    D   0.7

Common Core Standard 6.EE.B.7 – Expressions & Equations

☐   **The pack of 12 l contains x bottles of 1/2 l. Solve for x corresponding equation $\frac{1}{2}x = 12$. Be sure to show your work.**

    A   6

    B   10

    C   14

    D   24

Common Core Standard 6.EE.B.7 – Expressions & Equations

☐ A grasshopper is *x* in long. A bee is 1 in long, which is 1 1/4 in shorter than a grasshopper. Solve for *x* corresponding equation x - $1\frac{1}{4}$ = 1. Be sure to show your work.

A $\frac{1}{4}$

B $\frac{3}{4}$

C $1\frac{1}{4}$

D $2\frac{1}{4}$

Common Core Standard 6.EE.B.7 – Expressions & Equations

☐ Solve for *x* in the expression below. Be sure to show your work.

$$3.2 - x = 1.6$$

A   1.6

B   2.2

C   2.6

D   3.2

Common Core Standard 6.EE.B.7 – Expressions & Equations

☐ The perimeter of a square which side is *x* ft long is 0.8 ft. Solve for *x* corresponding equation *4x = 0.8*. Be sure to show your work.

A   0.2

B   0.32

C   3.2

D   20

Common Core Standard 6.EE.B.8 – Expressions & Equations

The average temperature in August was greater than $71^{\circ}F$. Which expression represents this situation? Be sure to show your work.

A $x < 71$

B $x > 71$

C $x = 71$

D $x + 71$

Common Core Standard 6.EE.B.8 – Expressions & Equations

Which expression is represented by the number line below? Be sure to show your work.

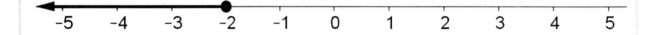

A $x < -2$

B $x = -2$

C $x > -2$

D $x - 2$

Common Core Standard 6.EE.B.8 – Expressions & Equations

The number of students in the class in the primary school must be less than 30. Which expression represents this situation? Be sure to show your work.

A $x = 30$

B $x - 30$

C $x > 30$

D $x < 30$

Common Core Standard 6.EE.B.8 – Expressions & Equations

☐ The number of passengers in the car must be less than 5. Which expression represents this situation? Be sure to show your work.

A   x = 5

B   x − 5

C   x < 5

D   x > 5

Common Core Standard 6.EE.B.8 – Expressions & Equations

☐ Which expression is represented by the number line below? Be sure to show your work.

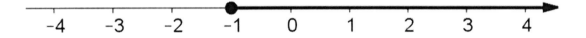

A   x < -1

B   x > -1

C   x − 1

D   x = -1

Common Core Standard 6.EE.B.8 – Expressions & Equations

☐ The number of soldiers in a squad is greater than 10. Which expression represents this situation? Be sure to show your work.

A   x > 10

B   x + 10

C   x = 10

D   x < 10

Name_____

Common Core Standard 6.EE.B.8 – Expressions & Equations

☐ The average weight of 9 years old children is greater than 80 lb. Which expression represents this situation? Be sure to show your work.

A   x > 9

B   x < 9

C   x > 80

D   x < 80

Common Core Standard 6.EE.B.8 – Expressions & Equations

☐ Which expression is represented by the number line below? Be sure to show your work.

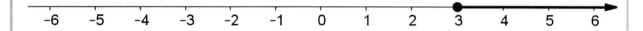

A   x < 3

B   x > 3

C   x < 6

D   x > 6

Common Core Standard 6.EE.B.8 – Expressions & Equations

☐ Franklin counted the number of kids of 6 families in the neighborhood. The average number of children per family is greater than 2. Which expression represents this situation?   Be sure to show your work.

A   x < 6

B   x > 6

C   x < 2

D   x > 2

Common Core Standard 6.EE.B.8 – Expressions & Equations

☐ **Irene spent more than $200 in 5 stores. Which expression represents this situation? Be sure to show your work.**

A   x > 200

B   x < 200

C   x > 5

D   x < 5

Common Core Standard 6.EE.B.8 – Expressions & Equations

☐ **Which expression is represented by the number line below? Be sure to show your work.**

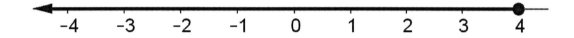

A   x > -4

B   x < -4

C   x > 4

D   x < 4

Common Core Standard 6.EE.B.8 – Expressions & Equations

☐ **Abraham served more than 12 peaches in 4 plates. Which expression represents this situation? Be sure to show your work.**

A   x < 12

B   x > 12

C   x < 4

D   x > 4

Name_____

Common Core Standard 6.EE.B.8 – Expressions & Equations

☐ **All of 25 employees in the post office are less than 2 m tall. Which expression represents this situation? Be sure to show your work.**

A   x < 2

B   x > 2

C   x < 25

D   x > 25

Common Core Standard 6.EE.B.8 – Expressions & Equations

☐ **Which expression is represented by the number line below? Be sure to show your work.**

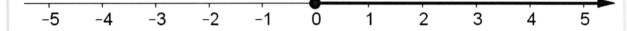

A   x > 5

B   x < 5

C   x > 0

D   x < 0

Common Core Standard 6.EE.B.8 – Expressions & Equations

☐ **The maximum number of points on the test is 20, and Isaac needed more than 16 points to qualify for the next level. Which expression represents this situation? Be sure to show your work.**

A   x < 20

B   x > 20

C   x < 16

D   x > 16

Common Core Standard 6.EE.B.8 – Expressions & Equations

☐ **In the group of 20 students more than a half are girls. Which expression represents this situation? Be sure to show your work.**

A $x > 20$

B $x < 20$

C $x > 10$

D $x < 10$

Common Core Standard 6.EE.B.8 – Expressions & Equations

☐ **Which expression is represented by the number line below? Be sure to show your work.**

A $x < -3$

B $x > -3$

C $x < 0$

D $x > 0$

Common Core Standard 6.EE.B.8 – Expressions & Equations

☐ **Less than 1/3 of 18 animals in the circus are from Africa. Which expression represents this situation? Be sure to show your work.**

A $x > \frac{1}{3}$

B $x > 3$

C $x < 6$

D $x < 18$

Common Core Standard 6.EE.B.8 – Expressions & Equations

☐ In the class of 24 students every 3rd student is a boy, which means that more than a half students are girls. Which expression represents this situation? Be sure to show your work.

A   x > 3

B   x < 3

C   x > 12

D   x < 24

Common Core Standard 6.EE.B.8 – Expressions & Equations

☐ Which expression is represented by the number line below? Be sure to show your work.

A   x < 8

B   x > 8

C   x < 4

D   x > 4

Common Core Standard 6.EE.B.8 – Expressions & Equations

☐ Less than a half of Earth's surface is covered by land. Which expression represents this situation? Be sure to show your work.

A $x - \frac{1}{2}$

B $x = \frac{1}{2}$

C $x > \frac{1}{2}$

D $x < \frac{1}{2}$

Name_____

Common Core Standard 6.EE.B.8 – Expressions & Equations

☐ **4 buildings in the street have more than 5 floors. Which expression represents this situation? Be sure to show your work.**

A   x > 4

B   x < 4

C   x > 5

D   x < 5

Common Core Standard 6.EE.B.8 – Expressions & Equations

☐ **Which expression is represented by the number line below? Be sure to show your work.**

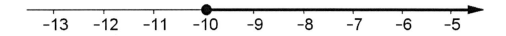

A   x > -10

B   x < -10

C   x > -5

D   x < -5

Common Core Standard 6.EE.B.8 – Expressions & Equations

☐ **Basketball team has 5 players. Football team has more players than basketball team. Which expression represents this situation? Be sure to show your work.**

A   x < 5

B   x > 5

C   x + 5

D   x = 5

Name_____

Common Core Standard 6.EE.C.9 – Expressions & Equations

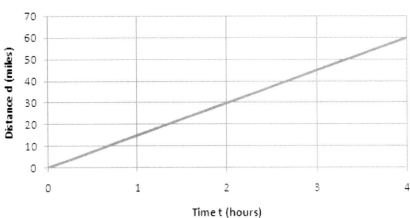

Bicycle ride

What is the equation of line in the graph above? Be sure to show your work.

A   d = 2t   C   t = 2d

B   d = 15t   D   t = 15d

Common Core Standard 6.EE.C.9 – Expressions & Equations

How many miles does bicycle pass after 3 hours? Be sure to show your work.

A   15   C   45

B   30   D   60

Common Core Standard 6.EE.C.9 – Expressions & Equations

How many hours does bicycle need to pass 30 miles? Be sure to show your work.

A   1   C   3

B   2   D   4

Common Core Standard 6.EE.C.9 – Expressions & Equations

Babysitting				
Week (w)	1	2	3	4
Earnings (e)	$400	$800	$1,200	$1,600

☐ **Which equation represents relationship between weeks and earnings in the table above? Be sure to show your work.**

A $w = 400e$

B $e = \dfrac{400}{w}$

C $w = \dfrac{400}{e}$

D $e = 400w$

Common Core Standard 6.EE.C.9 – Expressions & Equations

☐ **How much money does babysitter earn in 2 weeks? Be sure to show your work.**

A $400

B $800

C $1,200

D $1,600

Common Core Standard 6.EE.C.9 – Expressions & Equations

☐ **How many weeks does babysitter need to work to earn $400? Be sure to show your work.**

A   1

B   2

C   3

D   4

Common Core Standard 6.EE.C.9 – Expressions & Equations

"The pack of glasses contains 6 glasses."

Which equation represents the relationship between packs (p) and glasses (g)? Be sure to show your work.

A   p = g + 6

B   g = p + 6

C   p = 6g

D   g = 6p

Common Core Standard 6.EE.C.9 – Expressions & Equations

How many glasses do 4 packs contain? Be sure to show your work.

A   10

B   24

C   46

D   64

Common Core Standard 6.EE.C.9 – Expressions & Equations

Angela bought 18 glasses. How many packs did she buy? Be sure to show your work.

A   3

B   6

C   12

D   24

Common Core Standard 6.EE.C.9 – Expressions & Equations

The relationship between spiders (*s*) and the number of their legs (*l*) is given by the equation:
$$l = 8s$$

☐ How many spiders have 32 legs? Be sure to show your work.

A   2

B   4

C   6

D   8

Common Core Standard 6.EE.C.9 – Expressions & Equations

☐ How many legs do 3 spiders have? Be sure to show your work.

A   5

B   11

C   24

D   83

Common Core Standard 6.EE.C.9 – Expressions & Equations

☐ What is the least number of spiders who have more than 50 legs? Be sure to show your work.

A   4

B   5

C   6

D   7

Common Core Standard 6.EE.C.9 – Expressions & Equations

Taxi Cost

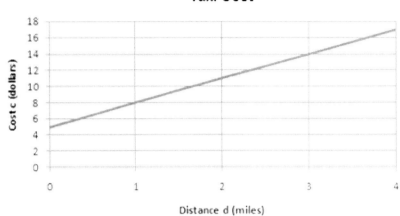

What is the equation of the line in the graph above? Be sure to show your work.

A $d = 3 + 5c$ C $d = 5 + 3c$

B $c = 3 + 5d$ D $c = 5 + 3d$

Common Core Standard 6.EE.C.9 – Expressions & Equations

How many miles one can drive by taxi with $14? Be sure to show your work.

A   1   C   3

B   2   D   4

Common Core Standard 6.EE.C.9 – Expressions & Equations

How much does taxi driver charge for a ride of 2 miles? Be sure to show your work.

A $8   C $14

B $11   D $17

Name_____

Common Core Standard 6.EE.C.9 – Expressions & Equations

Shoe Selling				
Hours (h)	1	2	3	4
Shoes in stock (s)	94	88	82	76

☐ **Which equation represents relationship between hours and shoes in stock in the table above? Be sure to show your work.**

A   s = 100 – 6h

B   h = 100 – 6s

C   s = 6h – 100

D   h = 6s – 100

Common Core Standard 6.EE.C.9 – Expressions & Equations

☐ **After how many hours is the number of shoes in stock 76? Be sure to show your work.**

A   1

B   2

C   3

D   4

Common Core Standard 6.EE.C.9 – Expressions & Equations

☐ **What is the number of shoes in stock after 2 hours? Be sure to show your work.**

A   76

B   82

C   88

D   94

Common Core Standard 6.EE.C.9 – Expressions & Equations

Lydia has $40 and she saves $10 every week.

☐ Which equation represents the relationship between the total savings (t) and a weekly savings (w)? Be sure to show your work.

A $t = 40w + 10$

B $w = 40t + 10$

C $t = 10w + 40$

D $w = 10t + 40$

Common Core Standard 6.EE.C.9 – Expressions & Equations

☐ How much money will Lydia have after 3 weeks? Be sure to show your work.

A $70

B $90

C $110

D $130

Common Core Standard 6.EE.C.9 – Expressions & Equations

☐ How many weeks does Lydia need to save $80?   Be sure to show your work.

A   4

B   5

C   6

D   7

Common Core Standard 6.EE.C.9 – Expressions & Equations

The relationship between cars produced (*c*) and the number of working hours (*h*) is given by the equation:

$$c = 6h - 2$$

☐ How many cars are produced after 8 hours? Be sure to show your work.

A   12

B   32

C   46

D   66

Common Core Standard 6.EE.C.9 – Expressions & Equations

☐ How many hours does production of 40 cars last? Be sure to show your work.

A   5

B   6

C   7

D   8

Common Core Standard 6.EE.C.9 – Expressions & Equations

☐ What is the least number of hours needed for production of more than 50 cars? Be sure to show your work.

A   6

B   7

C   8

D   9

Common Core Standard 6.G.A.1 – Geometry

☐ **What is the area of the floor in the picture below? Be sure to show your work.**

A   14 yd^2

B   20 yd^2

C   24 yd^2

D   30 yd^2

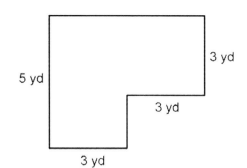

Common Core Standard 6.G.A.1 – Geometry

☐ **What is the area of the triangle below? Be sure to show your work.**

A   6 in^2

B   7 in^2

C   12 in^2

D   14 in^2

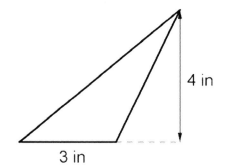

Common Core Standard 6.G.A.1 – Geometry

☐ **What is the area of the lot in the picture below? Be sure to show your work.**

A   26 yd^2

B   52 yd^2

C   72 yd^2

D   576 yd^2

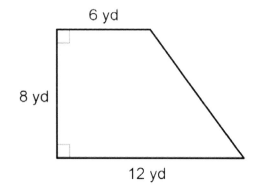

Common Core Standard 6.G.A.1 – Geometry

What is the area of a kite in the picture below? Be sure to show your work.

A   12 ft²

B   24 ft²

C   36 ft²

D   48 ft²

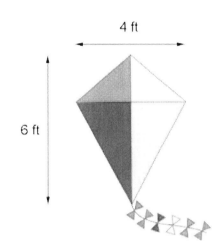

4 ft

6 ft

Common Core Standard 6.G.A.1 – Geometry

What is the area of the rhombus below? Be sure to show your work.

A   9 in²

B   10 in²

C   18 in²

D   20 in²

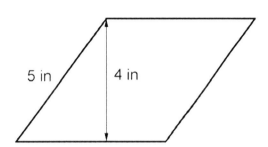

5 in   4 in

Common Core Standard 6.G.A.1 – Geometry

What is the area of an envelope in the picture below? Be sure to show your work.

A   12 in²

B   35 in²

C   57 in²

D   75 in²

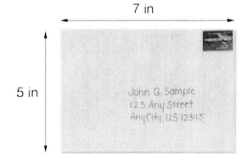

7 in

5 in

John G. Sample
123 Any Street
AnyCity, US 12345

Common Core Standard 6.G.A.1 – Geometry

What is the area of the tetris piece in the picture below? Be sure to show your work.

A 3 in²

B 4 in²

C 5 in²

D 6 in²

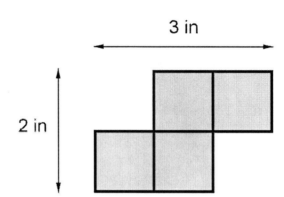

3 in

2 in

Common Core Standard 6.G.A.1 – Geometry

What is the area of the right triangle below? Be sure to show your work.

A 1 ft²

B 6 ft²

C 7 ft²

D 12 ft²

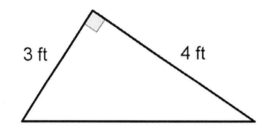

3 ft   4 ft

Common Core Standard 6.G.A.1 – Geometry

What is the area of the screen in the picture below? Be sure to show your work.

A 12 ft²

B 24 ft²

C 35 ft²

D 70 ft²

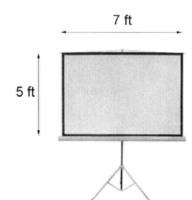

7 ft

5 ft

Name_____

Common Core Standard 6.G.A.1 – Geometry

☐ **What is the area of the swimming pool in the picture below? Be sure to show your work.**

A   18 m²

B   27 m²

C   31.5 m²

D   36 m²

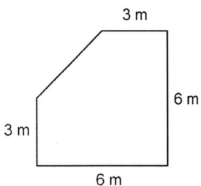

Common Core Standard 6.G.A.1 – Geometry

☐ **What is the area of an isosceles triangle below? Be sure to show your work.**

A   5 cm²

B   10 cm²

C   12 cm²

D   24 cm²

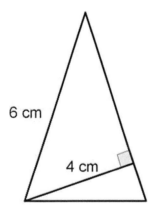

Common Core Standard 6.G.A.1 – Geometry

☐ **What is the area of the frame in the picture below? Be sure to show your work.**

A   4 ft²

B   15 ft²

C   20 ft²

D   35 ft²

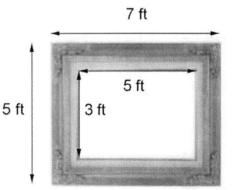

Common Core Standard 6.G.A.1 – Geometry

☐ **What is the area of the letter T in the picture below? Be sure to show your work.**

A   9 yd²

B   11 yd²

C   18 yd²

D   22 yd²

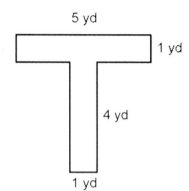

Common Core Standard 6.G.A.1 – Geometry

☐ **What is the area of the figure below? Be sure to show your work.**

A   6 in²

B   8 in²

C   12 in²

D   16 in²

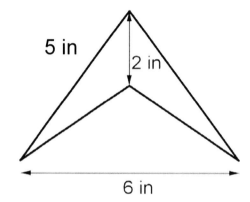

Common Core Standard 6.G.A.1 – Geometry

☐ **What is the area of the back side of the house in the picture below? Be sure to show your work.**

A   32 ft²

B   40 ft²

C   102 ft²

D   110 ft²

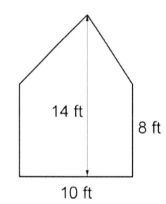

Name_____

☐ **What is the area of the dock in the picture below? Be sure to show your work.**

A 270 m²

B 297 m²

C 351 m²

D 378 m²

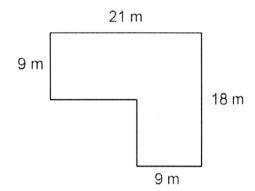

☐ **What is the area of the figure below? Be sure to show your work.**

A 13 cm²

B 21 cm²

C 42 cm²

D 84 cm²

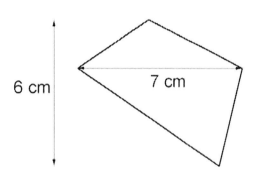

☐ **What is the area of the cross in the picture below (all edges are equal)? Be sure to show your work.**

A 8 ft²

B 10 ft²

C 16 ft²

D 20 ft²

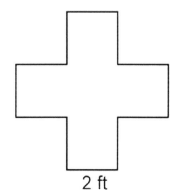

Common Core Standard 6.G.A.1 – Geometry

What is the area of the opened envelope in the picture below? Be sure to show your work.

A   120 in²

B   114 in²

C   96 in²

D   82 in²

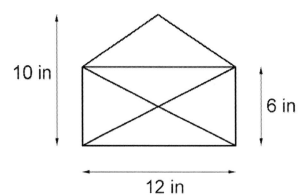

Common Core Standard 6.G.A.1 – Geometry

What is the area of the figure below? Be sure to show your work.

A   16 cm²

B   18 cm²

C   21 cm²

D   27 cm²

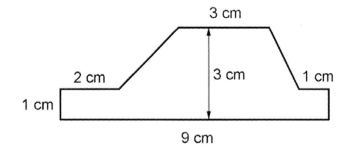

Common Core Standard 6.G.A.1 – Geometry

What is the area of the boat in the picture below? Be sure to show your work.

A   8 m²

B   16 m²

C   19 m²

D   24 m²

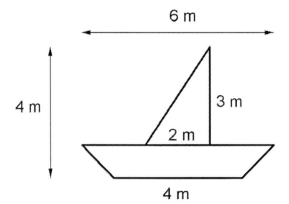

Name_____

Common Core Standard 6.G.A.1 – Geometry

☐ What is the area of the flashlight in the picture below? Be sure to show your work.

A   10 cm²

B   12 cm²

C   14 cm²

D   16 cm²

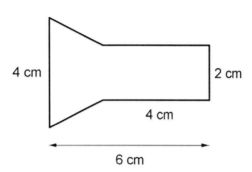

Common Core Standard 6.G.A.1 – Geometry

☐ What is the area of the figure to the right? Be sure to show your work.

A   6 cm²

B   9 cm²

C   12 cm²

D   18 cm²

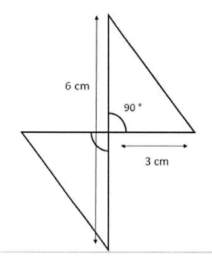

Common Core Standard 6.G.A.1 – Geometry

☐ What is the area of the hourglass in the picture below? Be sure to show your work.

A   6 in²

B   7 in²

C   12 in²

D   14 in²

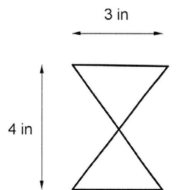

Name_____

Common Core Standard 6.G.A.2 – Geometry

 What is the volume of the box in the picture below? Be sure to show your work.

A $\frac{1}{4}$ m³

B $\frac{1}{3}$ m³

C $\frac{1}{2}$ m³

D   1 m³

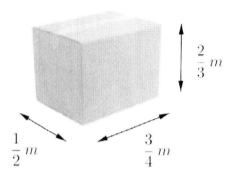

Common Core Standard 6.G.A.2 – Geometry

The prism is filled with unit cubes. What is the length of the edge of a unit cube? Be sure to show your work.

A $\frac{1}{2}$ ft

B $\frac{1}{3}$ ft

C $\frac{1}{4}$ ft

D $\frac{1}{6}$ ft

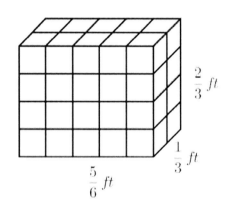

Common Core Standard 6.G.A.2 – Geometry

What is the volume of the aquarium in the picture below with the area of base 2/5 m²? Be sure to show your work.

A $\frac{5}{9}$ m³

B $\frac{3}{10}$ m³

C $\frac{1}{4}$ m³

D $\frac{2}{3}$ m³

Common Core Standard 6.G.A.2 – Geometry

☐ **What is the volume of the matchbox in the picture below? Be sure to show your work.**

A   3 in³

B $\frac{3}{2}$ in³

C   1 in³

D $\frac{3}{4}$ in³

Common Core Standard 6.G.A.2 – Geometry

☐ **The prism is filled with unit cubes. What is the length of the edge of a unit cube? Be sure to show your work.**

A $\frac{1}{2}$ yd

B $\frac{1}{4}$ yd

C $\frac{1}{6}$ yd

D $\frac{1}{8}$ yd

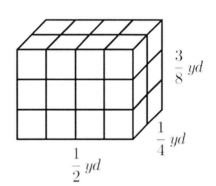

Common Core Standard 6.G.A.2 – Geometry

☐ **What is the volume of the sandbox in the picture below the area of which is 25/4 m² on the base? Be sure to show your work.**

A $\frac{25}{6}$ m³

B $\frac{27}{7}$ m³

C $\frac{50}{7}$ m³

D $\frac{9}{4}$ m³

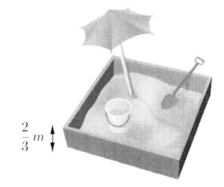

Name_____

Common Core Standard 6.G.A.2 – Geometry

☐ **What is the volume of the carton of milk in the picture below? Be sure to show your work.**

A $\frac{1}{18}$ ft^3

B $\frac{1}{9}$ ft^3

C $\frac{1}{6}$ ft^3

D $\frac{1}{3}$ ft^3

$1ft$

$\frac{1}{6} ft$ $\frac{1}{3} ft$

Common Core Standard 6.G.A.2 – Geometry

☐ **The prism is filled with unit cubes. What is the length of the edge of a unit cube? Be sure to show your work.**

A $\frac{1}{8}$ m

B $\frac{1}{6}$ m

C $\frac{1}{4}$ m

D $\frac{1}{2}$ m

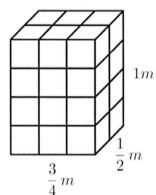

$1m$

$\frac{1}{2} m$

$\frac{3}{4} m$

Common Core Standard 6.G.A.2 – Geometry

☐ **What is the volume of the block of cheese in the picture below with the area of base 1/16 ft²? Be sure to show your work.**

A $\frac{1}{8}$ ft^3

B $\frac{1}{16}$ ft^3

C $\frac{1}{64}$ ft^3

D $\frac{1}{128}$ ft^3

$\frac{1}{8} ft$

Common Core Standard 6.G.A.2 – Geometry

☐ What is the volume of the box of ice cream in the picture below? Be sure to show your work.

A $\frac{1}{6}$ m³

B $\frac{1}{10}$ m³

C $\frac{1}{15}$ m³

D $\frac{1}{30}$ m³

Common Core Standard 6.G.A.2 – Geometry

☐ The prism is filled with unit cubes. What is the length of the edge of a unit cube? Be sure to show your work.

A   1 in

B $\frac{1}{2}$ in

C $\frac{1}{4}$ in

D $\frac{1}{5}$ in

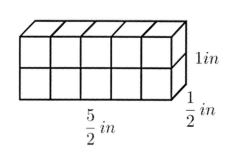

Common Core Standard 6.G.A.2 – Geometry

☐ What is the volume of the refrigerator in the picture below with the area of base 1/2 m²? Be sure to show your work.

A $\frac{3}{5}$ m³

B $\frac{1}{3}$ m³

C $\frac{2}{5}$ m³

D $\frac{1}{2}$ m³

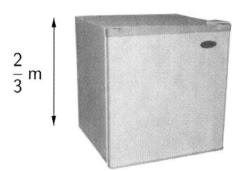

Common Core Standard 6.G.A.2 – Geometry

    What is the volume of the serving dish in the picture below? Be sure to show your work.

A $\frac{1}{8}$ m³

B $\frac{1}{6}$ m³

C $\frac{1}{4}$ m³

D $\frac{1}{2}$ m³

Common Core Standard 6.G.A.2 – Geometry

The prism is filled with unit cubes. What is the length of the edge of a unit cube? Be sure to show your work.

A $\frac{1}{2}$ cm

B $\frac{1}{3}$ cm

C $\frac{1}{6}$ cm

D $\frac{1}{8}$ cm

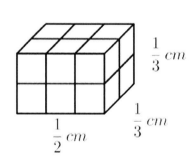

Common Core Standard 6.G.A.2 – Geometry

What is the volume of the flowerpot in the picture below which the area of base 1/3 yd²? Be sure to show your work.

A $\frac{3}{8}$ yd³

B $\frac{2}{15}$ yd³

C $\frac{1}{5}$ yd³

D $\frac{1}{4}$ yd³

Name_____

Common Core Standard 6.G.A.2 – Geometry

☐ What is the volume of the hamper in the picture below? Be sure to show your work.

A $\frac{11}{16}$ yd³

B $\frac{5}{8}$ yd³

C $\frac{3}{10}$ yd³

D $\frac{4}{11}$ yd³

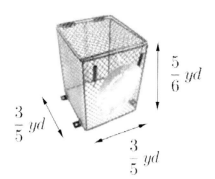

Common Core Standard 6.G.A.2 – Geometry

☐ The prism is filled with unit cubes. What is the length of the edge of a unit cube? Be sure to show your work.

A $\frac{1}{2}$ ft

B $\frac{1}{4}$ ft

C $\frac{1}{8}$ ft

D $\frac{1}{12}$ ft

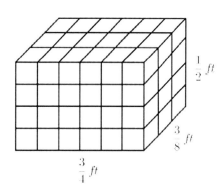

Common Core Standard 6.G.A.2 – Geometry

☐ What is the volume of the bucket in the picture below with the area of base 1/5 m²? Be sure to show your work.

A $\frac{3}{10}$ m³

B $\frac{2}{25}$ m³

C $\frac{1}{5}$ m³

D $\frac{4}{15}$ m³

Name_____

Common Core Standard 6.G.A.2 – Geometry

☐ **What is the volume of the ashtray in the picture below? Be sure to show your work.**

A $\frac{12}{49}$ yd³

B $\frac{8}{7}$ yd³

C $\frac{6}{7}$ yd³

D $\frac{8}{49}$ yd³

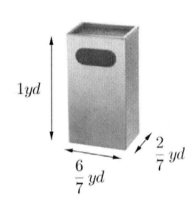

Common Core Standard 6.G.A.2 – Geometry

☐ **The prism is filled with unit cubes. What is the length of the edge of a unit cube? Be sure to show your work.**

A   1 in

B $\frac{1}{2}$ in

C $\frac{1}{4}$ in

D $\frac{1}{8}$ in

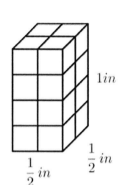

Common Core Standard 6.G.A.2 – Geometry

☐ **What is the volume of the brick in the picture below the area of base of which is 1/3 ft²? Be sure to show your work.**

A $\frac{1}{3}$ ft³

B $\frac{1}{6}$ ft³

C $\frac{1}{9}$ ft³

D $\frac{1}{27}$ ft³

Common Core Standard 6.G.A.2 – Geometry

☐ **What is the volume of the speaker in the picture below? Be sure to show your work.**

A $\frac{1}{3}$ ft³

B $\frac{1}{4}$ ft³

C $\frac{1}{6}$ ft³

D $\frac{1}{8}$ ft³

Common Core Standard 6.G.A.2 – Geometry

☐ **The prism is filled with unit cubes. What is the length of the length of the edge of a unit cube? Be sure to show your work.**

A 1 yd

B $\frac{1}{2}$ yd

C $\frac{1}{3}$ yd

D $\frac{1}{6}$ yd

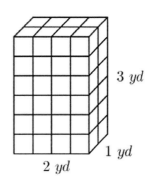

Common Core Standard 6.G.A.2 – Geometry

☐ **What is the volume of the ice in the picture below the area of base of which is 81/4 cm²? Be sure to show your work.**

A $\frac{45}{4}$ cm³

B 15 cm³

C 36 cm³

D $\frac{729}{8}$ cm³

Common Core Standard 6.G.A.3– Geometry

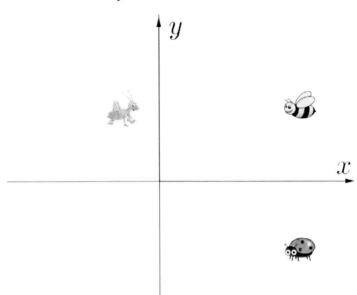

☐ **Look at the graph above. What is the distance between the bee (4,2) and the ladybug (4,-2)? Be sure to show your work.**

A   0   C   2

B   1   D   4

Common Core Standard 6.G.A.3– Geometry

☐ **What is the distance between the bee (4,2) and the grasshopper (-1,2)? Be sure to show your work.**

A   2   C   4

B   3   D   5

Common Core Standard 6.G.A.3– Geometry

☐ **What position should a fly be so that it forms a rectangle with the grasshopper (-1,2), the bee (4,2) and the ladybug (4,-2)? Be sure to show your work.**

A   (-1,-2)   C   (2,-2)

B   (-1,4)   D   (2,4)

Common Core Standard 6.G.A.3– Geometry

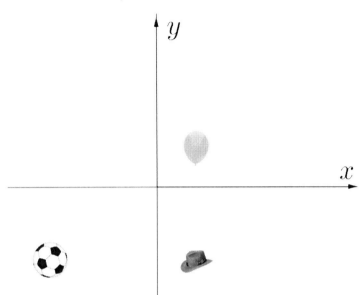

☐ Look at the graph above. What is the distance between the balloon (1,1) and the hat (1,-2)? Be sure to show your work.

A   1   C   3

B   2   D   4

Common Core Standard 6.G.A.3– Geometry

☐ What is the distance between the hat (1,-2) and the soccer ball (-3,-2)? Be sure to show your work.

A   1   C   3

B   2   D   4

Common Core Standard 6.G.A.3– Geometry

☐ Which point in the coordinate system forms a rectangle with the ball (-3,-2), the hat (1,-2) and the balloon (1,1)? Be sure to show your work.

A   (-2,1)   C   (1,-2)

B   (-3,1)   D   (1,-3)

Common Core Standard 6.G.A.3– Geometry

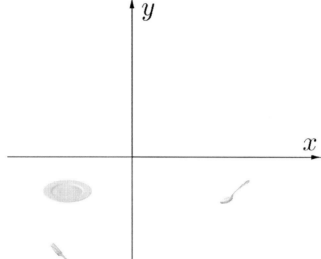

☐ **Look at the graph above. What is the distance between the plate (-2,-1) and the spoon (3,-1)? Be sure to show your work.**

A   1   C   5

B   2   D   6

Common Core Standard 6.G.A.3– Geometry

☐ **What is the distance between the plate (-2,-1) and the fork (-2,-3)? Be sure to show your work.**

A   1   C   3

B   2   D   4

Common Core Standard 6.G.A.3– Geometry

☐ **Which point in the coordinate system forms a rectangle with the spoon (3,-1), the plate (-2,-1) and the fork (-2,-3)? Be sure to show your work.**

A   (3,-2)   C   (-1,-2)

B   (3,-3)   D   (-1,-3)

Name_____

Common Core Standard 6.G.A.3– Geometry

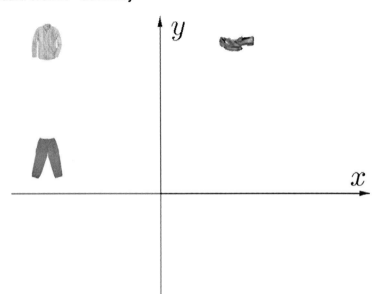

☐ **Look at the graph above. What is the distance between the pants (-3,1) and the shirt (-3,4)? Be sure to show your work.**

A   1   C   4

B   3   D   5

Common Core Standard 6.G.A.3– Geometry

☐ **What is the distance between the shoes (2,4) and the shirt (-3,4)? Be sure to show your work.**

A   2   C   4

B   3   D   5

Common Core Standard 6.G.A.3– Geometry

☐ **Which point in the coordinate system forms a rectangle with the shoes (2,4), the shirt (-3,4) and the pants (-3,1)? Be sure to show your work.**

A   (2,1)   C   (-3,2)

B   (-3,4)   D   (-4,-4)

Name_____

Common Core Standard 6.G.A.3– Geometry

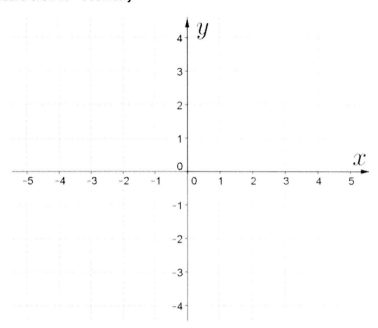

☐ **Draw points A(4,1), B(4,-2) and C(1,-2) in the coordinate plane above. What is the distance between A and B? Be sure to show your work.**

A   1   C   3

B   2   D   4

Common Core Standard 6.G.A.3– Geometry

☐ **What is the distance between B and C? Be sure to show your work.**

A   2   C   4

B   3   D   5

Common Core Standard 6.G.A.3– Geometry

☐ **Which point in the coordinate plane forms a rectangle with A, B and C? Be sure to show your work.**

A   (1,1)   C   (4,1)

B   (4,-2)   D   (1,-2)

Common Core Standard 6.G.A.3– Geometry

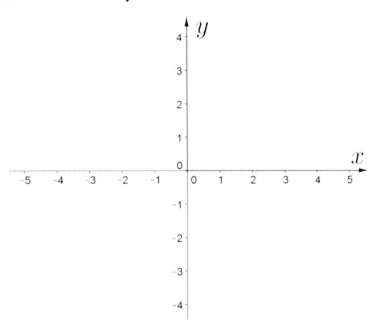

☐ **Draw points A(-3,0), B(-3,3) and C(1,3) in the coordinate plane above. What is the distance between A and B? Be sure to show your work.**

A	0		**C**	6
B	3		**D**	9

Common Core Standard 6.G.A.3– Geometry

☐ **What is the distance between B and C? Be sure to show your work.**

A	1		**C**	3
B	2		**D**	4

Common Core Standard 6.G.A.3– Geometry

☐ **Which point in the coordinate plane forms a rectangle with A, B and C? Be sure to show your work.**

A	(1,0)		**C**	(3,0)
B	(0,1)		**D**	(0,3)

Common Core Standard 6.G.A.3– Geometry

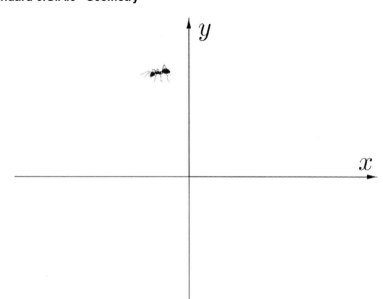

☐ **The position of the ant is (-1,3) in the graph above. What will the position of the ant be if it moves 4 units left parallel to x-axis? Be sure to show your work.**

A   (-1,-1)   C   (-5,3)

B   (-1,7)   D   (3,3)

Common Core Standard 6.G.A.3– Geometry

☐ **What will the position of the ant be if it moves 4 units up parallel to y-axis? Be sure to show your work.**

A   (-1,-1)   C   (-5,3)

B   (-1,7)   D   (3,3)

Common Core Standard 6.G.A.3– Geometry

☐ **What is the distance between the ant and the x-axis? Be sure to show your work.**

A   1   C   3

B   2   D   4

Common Core Standard 6.G.A.3– Geometry

☐ The position of the octopus is (-3,-2) in the graph above. What will the position of the octopus be if it moves 5 units right parallel to x-axis?   Be sure to show your work.

A   (2,-2)   C   (-3,3)

B   (-8,-2)   D   (-3,-7)

Common Core Standard 6.G.A.3– Geometry

☐ What will the position of the octopus be if it moves 5 units down parallel to y-axis? Be sure to show your work.

A   (2,-2)   C   (-3,3)

B   (-8,-2)   D   (-3,-7)

Common Core Standard 6.G.A.3– Geometry

☐ What is the distance between the octopus and the y-axis? Be sure to show your work.

A   1   C   3

B   2   D   5

Common Core Standard 6.G.A.4 – Geometry

☐   **What is the area of the pack of juice the net of which is shown in the picture below? Be sure to show your work.**

A   **2,000 cm²**

B   **2,200 cm²**

C   **2,400 cm²**

D   **2,600 cm²**

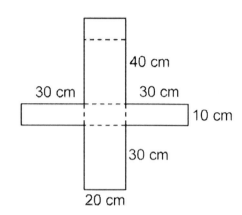

Common Core Standard 6.G.A.4 – Geometry

☐   **Which solid figure has the net shown in the picture below? Be sure to show your work.**

A   **Tetrahedron**

B   **Cube**

C   **Rectangular prism**

D   **Square pyramid**

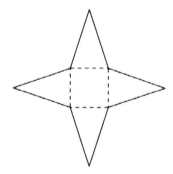

Common Core Standard 6.G.A.4 – Geometry

☐   **What is the area of the box the net of which is shown in the picture below? Be sure to show your work.**

A   **12 ft²**

B   **18 ft²**

C   **24 ft²**

D   **30 ft²**

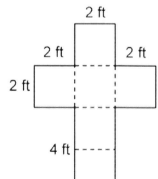

Name_____

Common Core Standard 6.G.A.4 – Geometry

☐ What is the area of the matchbox the net of which is shown in the picture below?   Be sure to show your work.

A   10 in²

B   16 in²

C   22 in²

D   28 in²

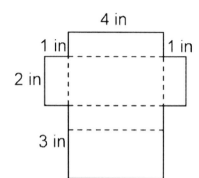

Common Core Standard 6.G.A.4 – Geometry

☐ Which solid figure has the net shown in the picture below? Be sure to show your work.

A   Tetrahedron

B   Cube

C   Rectangular prism

D   Square pyramid

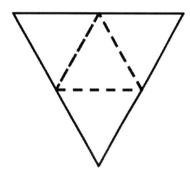

Common Core Standard 6.G.A.4 – Geometry

☐ What is the area of the pack of yogurt the net of wchich is shown in the picture below? Be sure to show your work.

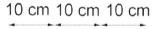

A   200 cm²

B   300 cm²

C   400 cm²

D   500 cm²

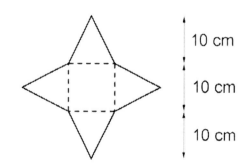

Name_____

Common Core Standard 6.G.A.4 – Geometry

☐ What is the area of the pack of pencils the net of which is shown in the picture below? Be sure to show your work.

A   32 in²

B   36 in²

C   40 in²

D   44 in²

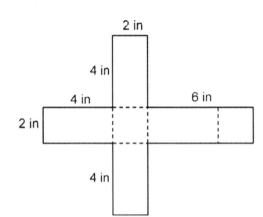

Common Core Standard 6.G.A.4 – Geometry

☐ Which solid figure has the net shown in the picture below? Be sure to show your work.

A   Tetrahedron

B   Cube

C   Rectangular prism

D   Square pyramid

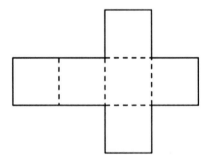

Common Core Standard 6.G.A.4 – Geometry

☐ What is the area of the pack of eggs the net of which is shown in the picture below? Be sure to show your work.

A $4\sqrt{3}$ in²

B $8\sqrt{3}$ in²

C $12\sqrt{3}$ in²

D $16\sqrt{3}$ in²

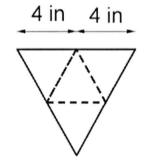

Common Core Standard 6.G.A.4 – Geometry

What is the area of the envelope the net of which is shown in the picture below? Be sure to show your work.

A   800 cm²

B   400 cm²

C   200 cm²

D   100 cm²

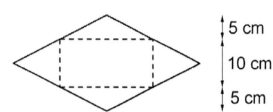

10 cm   20 cm   10 cm

5 cm
10 cm
5 cm

Common Core Standard 6.G.A.4 – Geometry

Which solid figure has the net shown in the picture below? Be sure to show your work.

A   Tetrahedron

B   Cube

C   Rectangular prism

D   Square pyramid

Common Core Standard 6.G.A.4 – Geometry

What is the area of the mailbox the net of which is shown in the picture below? Be sure to show your work.

A   6 ft²

B   9 ft²

C   12 ft²

D   13 ft²

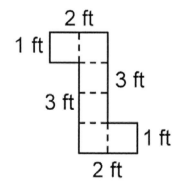

2 ft
1 ft
3 ft
3 ft
1 ft
2 ft

Name_____

Common Core Standard 6.G.A.4 – Geometry

☐ What is the area of the basket the net of which is shown in the picture below? Be sure to show your work.

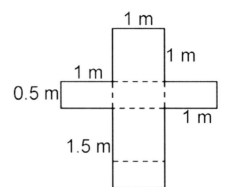

A   3 m²

B   4 m²

C   5 m²

D   6 m²

Common Core Standard 6.G.A.4 – Geometry

☐ Which figure consists of 6 squares? Be sure to show your work.

A   Pyramid

B   Tetrahedron

C   Cube

D   Rectangular prism

Common Core Standard 6.G.A.4 – Geometry

☐ What is the area of the milk pack the net of which is shown in the picture below?   Be sure to show your work.

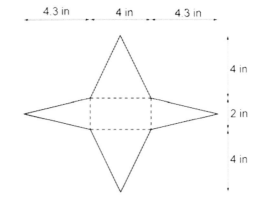

A   32.6 in²

B   33 in²

C   33.6 in²

D   34 in²

Name_____

Common Core Standard 6.G.A.4 – Geometry

☐ **What is the area of the cage the net of which is shown in the picture below? Be sure to show your work.**

A   16 ft²

B   20 ft²

C   24 ft²

D   28 ft²

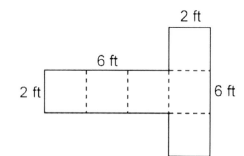

Common Core Standard 6.G.A.4 – Geometry

☐ **Which figure consists of equilateral triangles? Be sure to show your work.**

A   Pyramid

B   Tetrahedron

C   Cube

D   Rectangular prism

Common Core Standard 6.G.A.4 – Geometry

☐ **What is the area of the bucket the net of which is shown in the picture below? Be sure to show your work.**

A   608 in²

B   692 in²

C   708 in²

D   792 in²

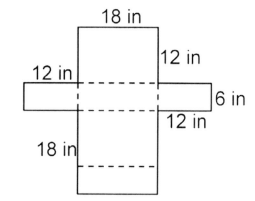

Name_____

Common Core Standard 6.G.A.4 – Geometry

☐ **What is the area of the pack of toothpicks with the net shown in the picture below? Be sure to show your work.**

A   44 cm²

B   56 cm²

C   88 cm²

D   112 cm²

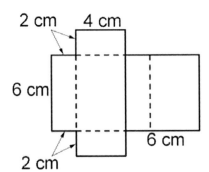

Common Core Standard 6.G.A.4 – Geometry

☐ **Which figure consists of triangles and quadrilaterals? Be sure to show your work.**

A   Pyramid

B   Tetrahedron

C   Cube

D   Rectangular prism

Common Core Standard 6.G.A.4 – Geometry

☐ **What is the area of the pack of creamer with net shown in the picture below? Be sure to show your work.**

A $4(1+\sqrt{3})$ in²

B $8(1+\sqrt{3})$ in²

C $16(1+\sqrt{3})$ in²

D $32(1+\sqrt{3})$ in²

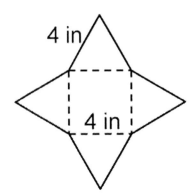

Common Core Standard 6.G.A.4 – Geometry

☐ **What is the area of the first aid kit with net shown in the picture below? Be sure to show your work.**

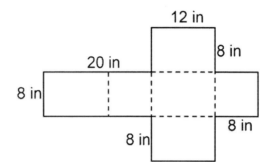

A   **512 in²**

B   **612 in²**

C   **712 in²**

D   **812 in²**

Common Core Standard 6.G.A.4 – Geometry

☐ **Which figure consists of rectangles? Be sure to show your work.**

A   **Pyramid**

B   **Tetrahedron**

C   **Cube**

D   **Rectangular prism**

Common Core Standard 6.G.A.4 – Geometry

☐ **What is the area of the box the net of which is shown in the picture below? Be sure to show your work.**

A   **10 m²**

B   **12 m²**

C   **20 m²**

D   **24 m²**

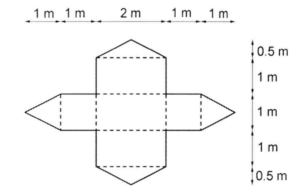

Name_____

Common Core Standard 6.SP.A.1 – Statistics & Probability

Student	Age	Height	Weight
George	12	165 cm	50 kg
Sonia	11	154 cm	48 kg
Michael	13	162 cm	52 kg
Ava	12	158 cm	49 kg
Peter	14	171 cm	63 kg
Maya	10	148 cm	42 kg

☐ **Look at the table above. Which of the following is NOT a statistical question?**

A   How old is Sonia?

B   How old are boys?

C   How old are girls?

D   How old are students?

Common Core Standard 6.SP.A.1 – Statistics & Probability

☐ **Which of the following is NOT a statistical question?**

A   How tall are boys?

B   How tall are girls?

C   How tall is Peter?

D   How tall are students?

Common Core Standard 6.SP.A.1 – Statistics & Probability

☐ **Which of the following is NOT a statistical question?**

A   How much do boys weigh?

B   How much does Michael weigh?

C   How much do girls weigh?

D   How much do students weigh?

Common Core Standard 6.SP.A.1 – Statistics & Probability

Soccer player	Age	Salary per week	Goals
Ethan	24	$6,000	1
Andrew	31	$10,000	3
Logan	26	$8,000	2
Christian	21	$11,000	6
Riley	34	$24,000	8
Cameron	23	$18,000	5

☐ Look at the table above. Which of the following is NOT a statistical question?

A   How old are players with earnings above $10,000 per week?

B   How old is Logan?

C   How old are players with earnings below $12,000 per week?

D   How old are players?

Common Core Standard 6.SP.A.1 – Statistics & Probability

☐ Which of the following is NOT a statistical question?

A   How much do players older than 30 years earn per week?

B   How much do players younger than 30 years earn per week?

C   How much does Riley earn per week?

D   How much do players earn per week?

Common Core Standard 6.SP.A.1 – Statistics & Probability

☐ Which of the following is NOT a statistical question?

A   How many goals did Ethan score?

B   How many goals did players older than 25 years score?

C   How many goals did players score?

D   How many goals did players younger than 25 years score?

Common Core Standard 6.SP.A.1 – Statistics & Probability

Employee	Age	Work hours per week	Absence (days)
Sarah	24	40	10
Kyle	31	20	18
Isabelle	26	30	15
Robert	21	25	12
Gabrielle	34	35	16
Blake	23	10	13

☐ Look at the table above. Which of the following is NOT a statistical question?

A   How old are the female employees?

B   How old are the male employees?

C   How old is Isabelle?

D   How old are the employees?

Common Core Standard 6.SP.A.1 – Statistics & Probability

☐ Which of the following is NOT a statistical question?

A   How many hours per week does Robert work?

B   How many hours per week do females work?

C   How many hours per week do males work?

D   How many hours per week do employees work?

Common Core Standard 6.SP.A.1 – Statistics & Probability

☐ Which of the following is NOT a statistical question?

A   How many days are female employees absent?

B   How many days are male employees absent?

C   How many days are employees absent?

D   How many days is Kyle absent?

Common Core Standard 6.SP.A.1 – Statistics & Probability

Teacher	Years of experience	Number of subjects taught	Head of department
Katelyn	23	2	Yes
Carson	12	1	No
Alexandra	34	3	No
Aaron	4	1	Yes
Jasmine	8	2	No
Chase	11	1	No

☐ Look at the table above. Which of the following is NOT a statistical question?

A   How many years of experience do heads of department have?

B   How many years of experience do females have?

C   How many years of experience do teachers have?

D   How many years of experience does Carson have?

Common Core Standard 6.SP.A.1 – Statistics & Probability

☐ Which of the following is NOT a statistical question?

A   How many subjects do females teach?

B   How many subjects does Jasmine teach?

C   How many subjects do males teach?

D   How many subjects do heads of departments teach?

Common Core Standard 6.SP.A.1 – Statistics & Probability

☐ Which of the following is NOT a statistical question?

A   Is Alexandra a head of department?

B   How many females are head of department?

C   How many males are head of department?

D   How many teachers are head of department?

Common Core Standard 6.SP.A.1 – Statistics & Probability

Doctor	Age	Salary per week	Years of experience
Angelina	42	$5,000	12
Peter	55	$8,000	30
Mia	51	$6,000	23
Jordan	27	$2,000	3
Arin	39	$4,000	14
Parker	30	$3,000	6

Look at the table above. Which of the following is NOT a statistical question?

A   How old are doctors with earnings above $5,000 per week?

B   How old are doctors?

C   How old are doctors with earnings below $5,000 per week?

D   How old is Arin?

Common Core Standard 6.SP.A.1 – Statistics & Probability

Which of the following is NOT a statistical question?

A   How much do doctors with more than 20 years of experience earn?

B   How much does Parker earn?

C   How much do doctors with less than 20 years of experience earn?

D   How much do doctors earn?

Common Core Standard 6.SP.A.1 – Statistics & Probability

Which of the following is NOT a statistical question?

A   How many years of experience do females have?

B   How many years of experience do males have?

C   How many years of experience does Angelina have?

D   How many years of experience do doctors have?

Common Core Standard 6.SP.A.1 – Statistics & Probability

Boxer	Age	Height	Weight
Ivan	24	172 cm	72 kg
Maxwell	22	168 cm	64 kg
Colin	27	164 cm	66 kg
Bryson	29	181 cm	90 kg
Henry	32	175 cm	83 kg
Justin	21	183 cm	81 kg

☐ **Look at the table above. Which of the following is NOT a statistical question?**

A   How old is Maxwell?

B   How old are boxers taller than 170 cm?

C   How old are boxers shorter than 170 cm?

D   How old are boxers?

Common Core Standard 6.SP.A.1 – Statistics & Probability

☐ **Which of the following is NOT a statistical question?**

A   How tall are boxers?

B   How tall are boxers older than 25 years?

C   How tall are boxers younger than 25 years?

D   How tall is Henry?

Common Core Standard 6.SP.A.1 – Statistics & Probability

☐ **Which of the following is NOT a statistical question?**

A   How much do boxers weigh?

B   How much do boxers older than 26 years weigh?

C   How much does Colin weigh?

D   How much do boxers taller than 172 cm weigh?

Common Core Standard 6.SP.A.1 – Statistics & Probability

Child	Age	Notebook	Pencil
Mason	6	5	3
Lusine	8	9	5
Joshua	7	8	4
Elizabeth	5	4	2
Nathan	7	7	6
Taylor	8	10	3

☐ Look at the table above. Which of the following is NOT a statistical question?

A How old are girls?

B How old are children?

C How old are boys?

D How old is Lusine?

Common Core Standard 6.SP.A.1 – Statistics & Probability

☐ Which of the following is NOT a statistical question?

A How many notebooks do boys have?

B How many notebooks do children have?

C How many notebooks does Nathan have?

D How many notebooks do girls have?

Common Core Standard 6.SP.A.1 – Statistics & Probability

☐ Which of the following is NOT a statistical question?

A How many pencils does Taylor have?

B How many pencils do boys have?

C How many pencils do girls have?

D How many pencils do children have?

Common Core Standard 6.SP.A.1 – Statistics & Probability

Tourist	Age	Nights	Price per night
Joseph	32	10	$40
Samantha	28	12	$30
Owen	36	9	$25
Morgan	19	11	$45
William	26	14	$50
Chloe	38	7	$35

☐ Look at the table above. Which of the following is NOT a statistical question?

A How old are tourists?

B How old are females?

C How old is Owen?

D How old are males?

Common Core Standard 6.SP.A.1 – Statistics & Probability

☐ Which of the following is NOT a statistical question?

A How many nights do males stay?

B How many nights do females stay?

C How many nights do tourists stay?

D How many nights does William stay?

Common Core Standard 6.SP.A.1 – Statistics & Probability

☐ Which of the following is NOT a statistical question?

A How much does Samantha pay per night?

B How much do tourists pay per night?

C How much do females pay per night?

D How much do males pay per night?

Name_____

Common Core Standard 6.SP.A.2 – Statistics & Probability

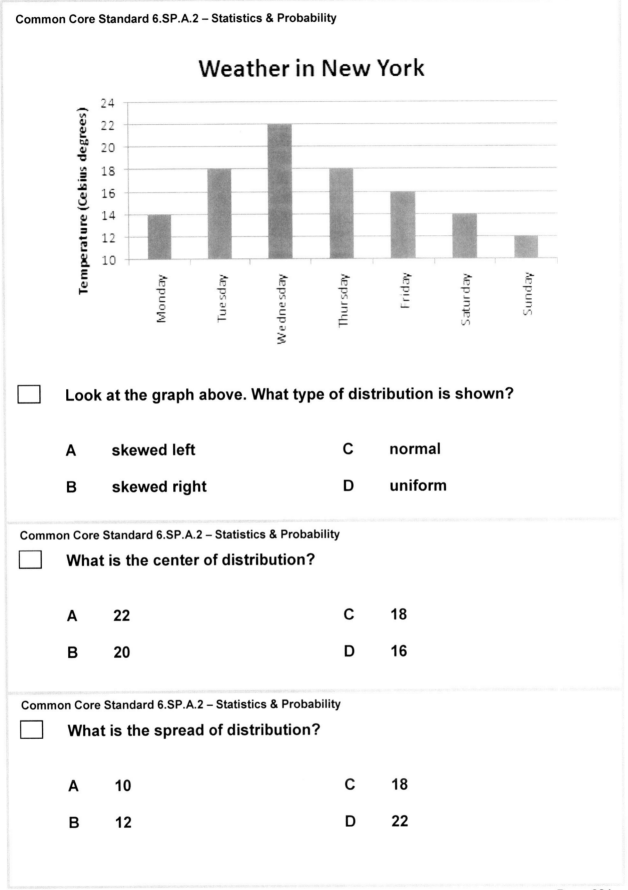

Weather in New York

☐ **Look at the graph above. What type of distribution is shown?**

A	**skewed left**	**C**	**normal**
B	**skewed right**	**D**	**uniform**

Common Core Standard 6.SP.A.2 – Statistics & Probability

☐ **What is the center of distribution?**

A	**22**	**C**	**18**
B	**20**	**D**	**16**

Common Core Standard 6.SP.A.2 – Statistics & Probability

☐ **What is the spread of distribution?**

A	**10**	**C**	**18**
B	**12**	**D**	**22**

Name_____

Common Core Standard 6.SP.A.2 – Statistics & Probability

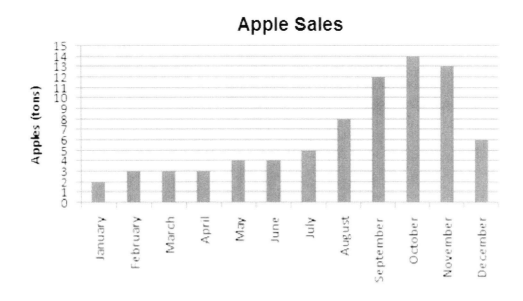

☐ Look at the graph above. What type of distribution is shown?

A   skewed left   C   normal

B   skewed right   D   uniform

Common Core Standard 6.SP.A.2 – Statistics & Probability

☐ What is the center of distribution?

A   4   C   7

B   4.5   D   7.5

Common Core Standard 6.SP.A.2 – Statistics & Probability

☐ What is the spread of distribution?

A   10   C   14

B   12   D   15

Name_____

Common Core Standard 6.SP.A.2 – Statistics & Probability

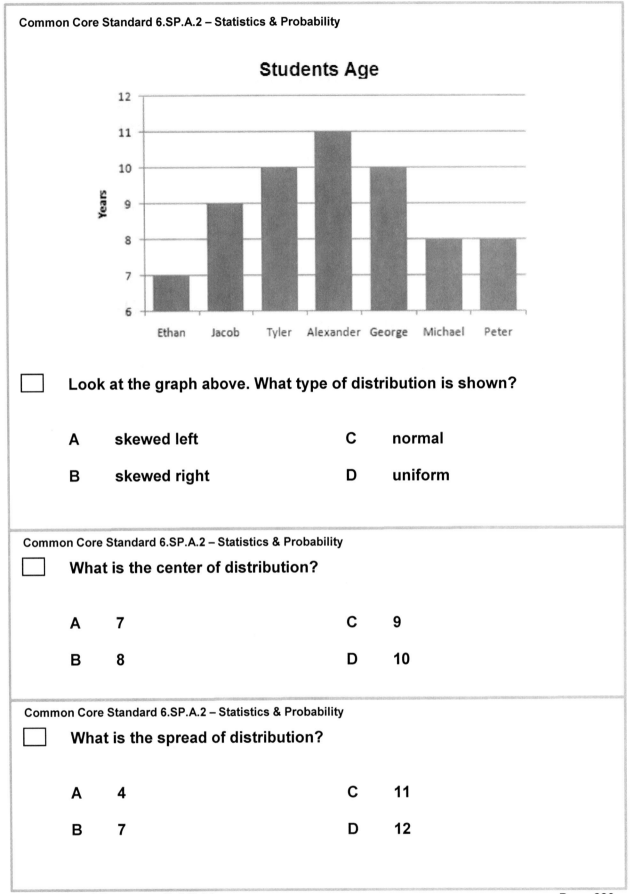

Students Age

☐ Look at the graph above. What type of distribution is shown?

A   skewed left   C   normal

B   skewed right   D   uniform

Common Core Standard 6.SP.A.2 – Statistics & Probability

☐ **What is the center of distribution?**

A   7   C   9

B   8   D   10

Common Core Standard 6.SP.A.2 – Statistics & Probability

☐ **What is the spread of distribution?**

A   4   C   11

B   7   D   12

Common Core Standard 6.SP.A.2 – Statistics & Probability

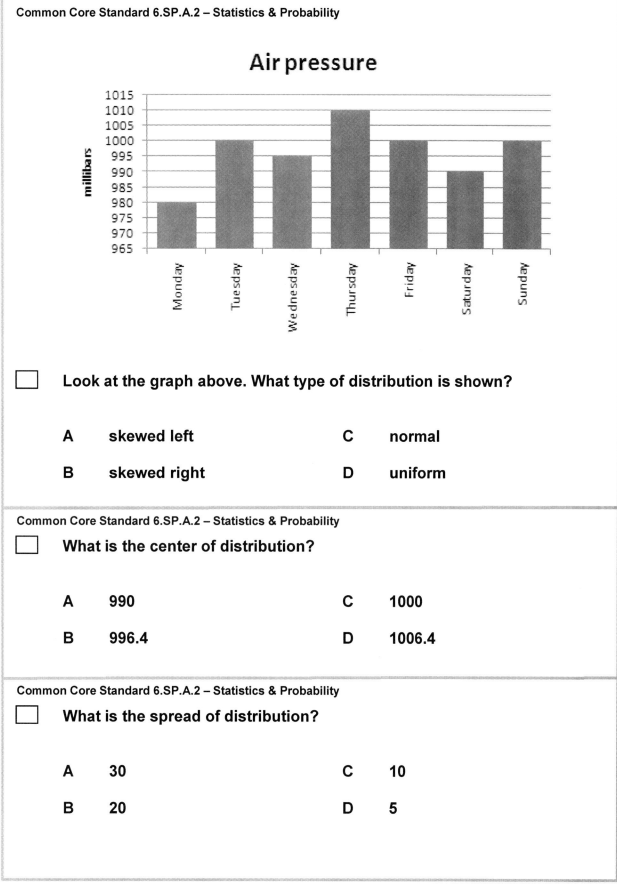

☐ Look at the graph above. What type of distribution is shown?

A   skewed left   C   normal

B   skewed right   D   uniform

Common Core Standard 6.SP.A.2 – Statistics & Probability

☐ What is the center of distribution?

A   990   C   1000

B   996.4   D   1006.4

Common Core Standard 6.SP.A.2 – Statistics & Probability

☐ What is the spread of distribution?

A   30   C   10

B   20   D   5

Common Core Standard 6.SP.A.2 – Statistics & Probability

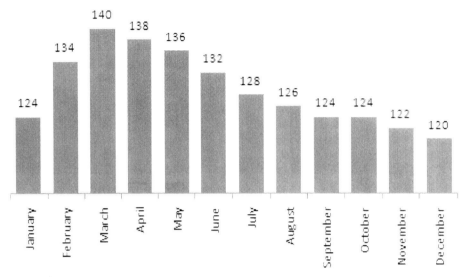

Mia's weight (pounds)

124 134 140 138 136 132 128 126 124 124 122 120

January February March April May June July August September October November December

Look at the graph above. What type of distribution is shown?

A   uniform   C   skewed right

B   normal   D   skewed left

Common Core Standard 6.SP.A.2 – Statistics & Probability

What is the center of distribution?

A   126   C   128

B   127   D   129

Common Core Standard 6.SP.A.2 – Statistics & Probability

What is the spread of distribution?

A   10   C   30

B   20   D   40

Common Core Standard 6.SP.A.2 – Statistics & Probability

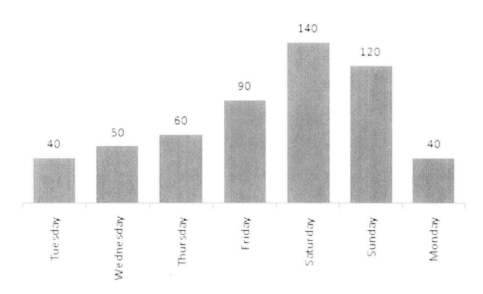

Cafe Guests

140

120

90

60

50

40   40

Tuesday   Wednesday   Thursday   Friday   Saturday   Sunday   Monday

☐ **Look at the graph above. What type of distribution is shown?**

A   uniform   C   skewed right

B   normal   D   skewed left

Common Core Standard 6.SP.A.2 – Statistics & Probability

☐ **What is the center of distribution?**

A   60   C   80

B   70   D   90

Common Core Standard 6.SP.A.2 – Statistics & Probability

☐ **What is the spread of distribution?**

A   40   C   100

B   80   D   140

Common Core Standard 6.SP.A.2 – Statistics & Probability

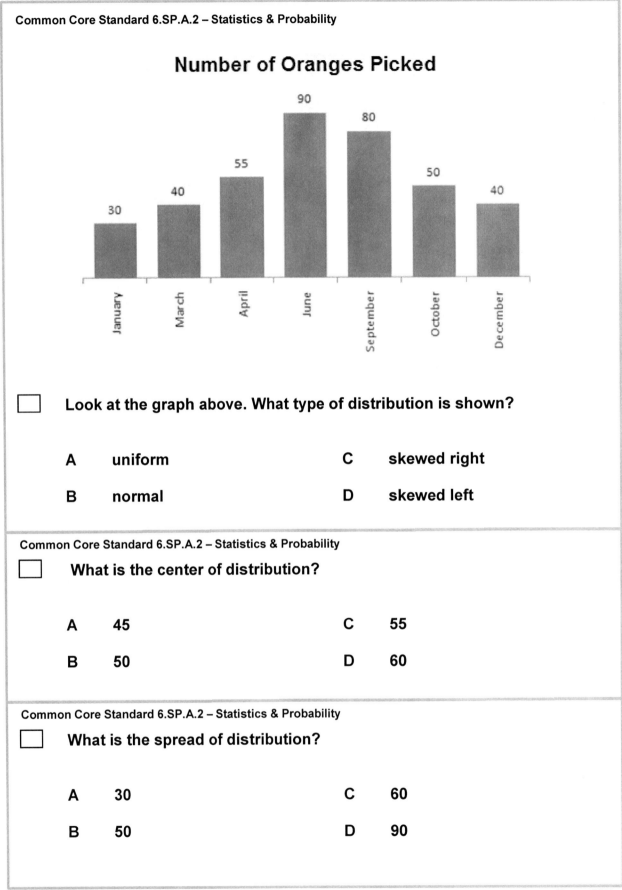

Number of Oranges Picked

☐ Look at the graph above. What type of distribution is shown?

A   uniform   C   skewed right

B   normal   D   skewed left

Common Core Standard 6.SP.A.2 – Statistics & Probability

☐ What is the center of distribution?

A   45   C   55

B   50   D   60

Common Core Standard 6.SP.A.2 – Statistics & Probability

☐ What is the spread of distribution?

A   30   C   60

B   50   D   90

Name_____

Common Core Standard 6.SP.A.2 – Statistics & Probability

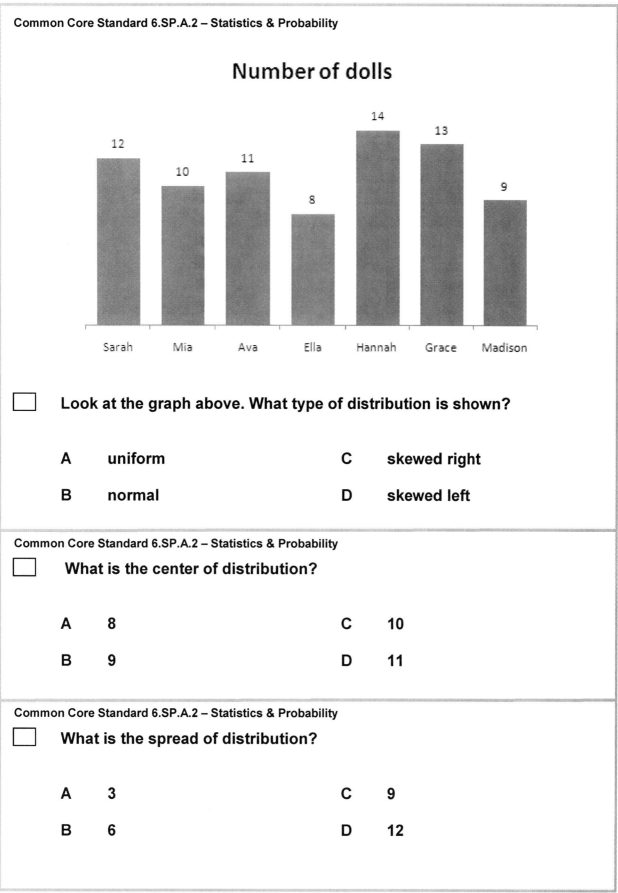

Number of dolls

☐ **Look at the graph above. What type of distribution is shown?**

A	uniform	C	skewed right
B	normal	D	skewed left

Common Core Standard 6.SP.A.2 – Statistics & Probability

☐ **What is the center of distribution?**

A	8	C	10
B	9	D	11

Common Core Standard 6.SP.A.2 – Statistics & Probability

☐ **What is the spread of distribution?**

A	3	C	9
B	6	D	12

Name_____

Common Core Standard 6.SP.A.3 – Statistics & Probability

Auto Dealership

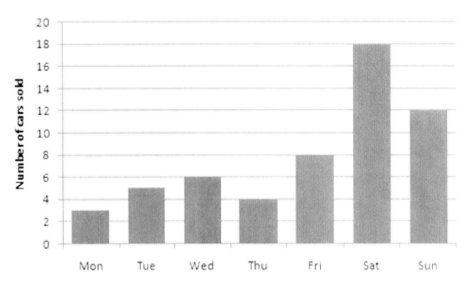

Look at the graph above. What is the mean of the data?

A   6   C   8

B   7   D   9

Common Core Standard 6.SP.A.3 – Statistics & Probability

What is the median of the data?

A   6   C   8

B   7   D   9

Common Core Standard 6.SP.A.3 – Statistics & Probability

What is the range of the data?

A   3   C   18

B   15   D   20

Common Core Standard 6.SP.A.3 – Statistics & Probability

Hasmik's Reading Book

Day	Monday	Tuesday	Wednesday	Thursday	Friday
Number of pages read	24	18	32	26	15

☐ Look at the table above. What is the mean of the data?

A   21

B   22

C   23

D   24

Common Core Standard 6.SP.A.3 – Statistics & Probability

☐ What is the median of the data?

A   21

B   22

C   23

D   24

Common Core Standard 6.SP.A.3 – Statistics & Probability

☐ What is the range of the data?

A   16

B   17

C   18

D   19

Common Core Standard 6.SP.A.3 – Statistics & Probability

Number of students per grade

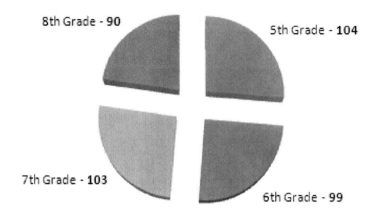

8th Grade - 90

5th Grade - 104

7th Grade - 103

6th Grade - 99

☐ Look at the graph above. What is the mean of the data?

A 98

C 100

B 99

D 101

Common Core Standard 6.SP.A.3 – Statistics & Probability

☐ What is the median of the data?

A 98

C 100

B 99

D 101

Common Core Standard 6.SP.A.3 – Statistics & Probability

☐ What is the range of the data?

A 5

C 13

B 9

D 14

Common Core Standard 6.SP.A.3 – Statistics & Probability

Rhea roles a dice

1, 6, 3, 4, 5, 5

☐ **Look at the data above. What is the mean of the data?**

A   3.5

B   4

C   4.5

D   5

Common Core Standard 6.SP.A.3 – Statistics & Probability

☐ **What is the median of the data?**

A   3.5

B   4

C   4.5

D   5

Common Core Standard 6.SP.A.3 – Statistics & Probability

☐ **What is the range of the data?**

A   3.5

B   4

C   4.5

D   5

Name_____

Common Core Standard 6.SP.A.3 – Statistics & Probability

Points scored

Connor

Nathan

Nicholas

Joshua

Mason

= 2 points

☐ **Look at the pictograph above. What is the mean of the data?**

A	8	C	10
B	9	D	11

Common Core Standard 6.SP.A.3 – Statistics & Probability

☐ **What is the median of the data?**

A	8	C	10
B	9	D	11

Common Core Standard 6.SP.A.3 – Statistics & Probability

☐ **What is the range of the data?**

A	8	C	12
B	10	D	14

Common Core Standard 6.SP.A.3 – Statistics & Probability

Number of sunny days

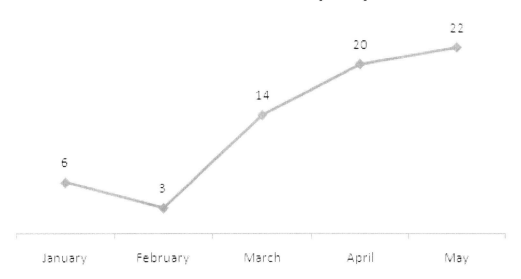

| | 6 | 3 | 14 | 20 | 22 |
| January | February | March | April | May |

☐ **Look at the graph above. What is the mean of the data?**

| A | 12 | C | 14 |
| B | 13 | D | 15 |

Common Core Standard 6.SP.A.3 – Statistics & Probability

☐ **What is the median of the data?**

| A | 12 | C | 14 |
| B | 13 | D | 15 |

Common Core Standard 6.SP.A.3 – Statistics & Probability

☐ **What is the range of the data?**

| A | 8 | C | 19 |
| B | 16 | D | 22 |

Common Core Standard 6.SP.A.3 – Statistics & Probability

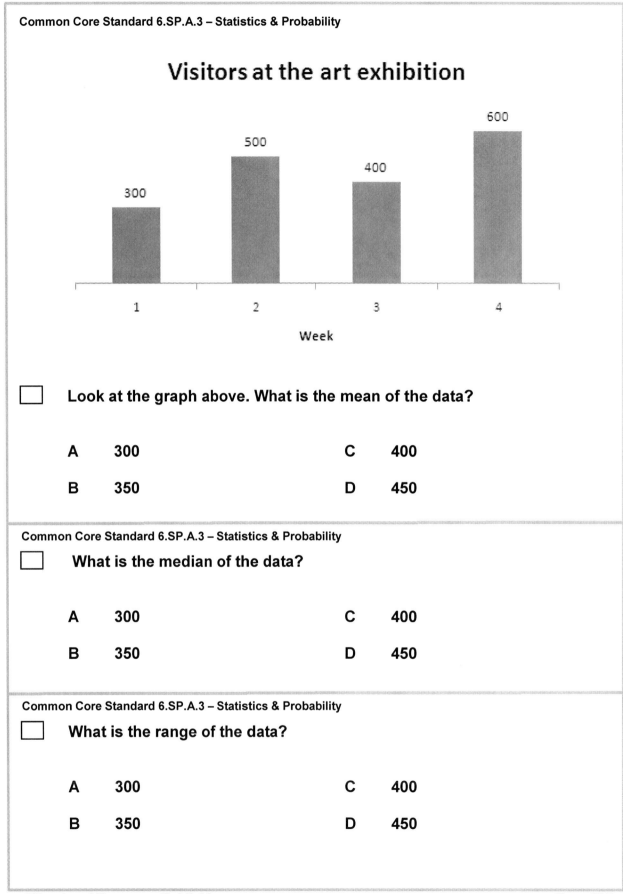

Look at the graph above. What is the mean of the data?

A   300   C   400

B   350   D   450

Common Core Standard 6.SP.A.3 – Statistics & Probability

What is the median of the data?

A   300   C   400

B   350   D   450

Common Core Standard 6.SP.A.3 – Statistics & Probability

What is the range of the data?

A   300   C   400

B   350   D   450

Common Core Standard 6.SP.A.3 – Statistics & Probability

Working hours per week

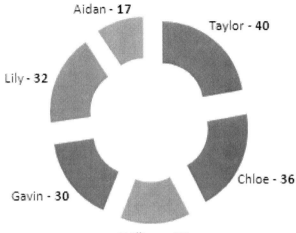

Aidan - 17

Taylor - 40

Lily - 32

Chloe - 36

Gavin - 30

William - 25

☐ **Look at the graph above. What is the mean of the data?**

A   28   C   30

B   29   D   31

Common Core Standard 6.SP.A.3 – Statistics & Probability

☐ **What is the median of the data?**

A   28   C   30

B   29   D   31

Common Core Standard 6.SP.A.3 – Statistics & Probability

☐ **What is the range of the data?**

A   23   C   25

B   24   D   26

Name_____

Common Core Standard 6.SP.A.4 – Statistics & Probability

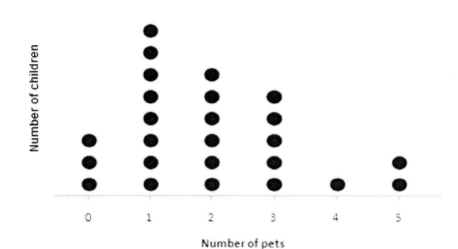

Children with Pets

Number of children

Number of pets

☐ **Look at the dot plot above. How many children have pets?**

A   16   C   22

B   19   D   25

Common Core Standard 6.SP.A.4 – Statistics & Probability

☐ **How many children have exactly 2 pets?**

A   3   C   5

B   4   D   6

Common Core Standard 6.SP.A.4 – Statistics & Probability

☐ **How many children have at least 3 pets?**

A   17   C   14

B   19   D   5

Name_____

Common Core Standard 6.SP.A.4 – Statistics & Probability

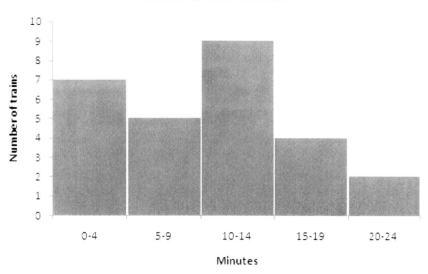

Look at the histogram above. How many trains are late less than 10 minutes?

A   5   C   9

B   7   D   12

Common Core Standard 6.SP.A.4 – Statistics & Probability

How many trains are late more than 15 minutes?

A   2   C   6

B   4   D   8

Common Core Standard 6.SP.A.4 – Statistics & Probability

How many trains are late between 10 and 15 minutes?

A   4   C   7

B   5   D   9

Common Core Standard 6.SP.A.4 – Statistics & Probability

Number of children on the playground from 9 a.m. to 5 p.m.

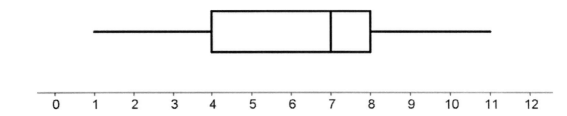

☐ **Look at the box plot above. What was the maximum number of children on the playground?**

A   7   C   11

B   8   D   12

Common Core Standard 6.SP.A.4 – Statistics & Probability

☐ **What was the minimum number of children on the playground?**

A   0   C   4

B   1   D   7

Common Core Standard 6.SP.A.4 – Statistics & Probability

☐ **What is the median of the data in the box plot?**

A   4   C   7

B   6   D   8

Name_____

PRACTICE

Common Core Standard 6.SP.A.4 – Statistics & Probability

Rolling dice

☐ Look at the dot plot above. How many times an even number has occurred?

A   13   C   9

B   11   D   7

Common Core Standard 6.SP.A.4 – Statistics & Probability

☐ How many times an odd has number occurred?

A   13   C   9

B   11   D   7

Common Core Standard 6.SP.A.4 – Statistics & Probability

☐ How many times has the number 2 occurred?

A   8   C   4

B   6   D   2

Name_____

Common Core Standard 6.SP.A.4 – Statistics & Probability

Hours Watching TV per Week

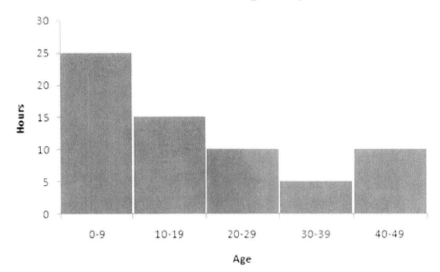

☐ Look at the histogram above. How many hours per week do people older than 30 years watch TV?

A 5

C 15

B 10

D 20

Common Core Standard 6.SP.A.4 – Statistics & Probability

☐ How many hours per week do people younger than 20 years watch TV?

A 40

C 60

B 45

D 65

Common Core Standard 6.SP.A.4 – Statistics & Probability

☐ How many hours per week do people watch TV?

A 50

C 60

B 55

D 65

Temperature in April (in Celsius)

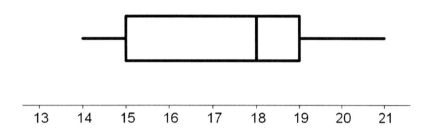

| 13 | 14 | 15 | 16 | 17 | 18 | 19 | 20 | 21 |

☐ Look at the box plot above. What was the highest temperature of the air measured in April?

A   15   C   19

B   18   D   21

☐ What was the lowest temperature of the air measured in April?

A   13   C   15

B   14   D   18

☐ What is the median of the data in the box plot?

A   15   C   18

B   17   D   19

Common Core Standard 6.SP.A.4 – Statistics & Probability

Goals Scored

Number of Players

Number of goals

☐ **Look at the dot plot above. How many soccer players have scored more than 3 goals?**

A   1   C   3

B   2   D   4

Common Core Standard 6.SP.A.4 – Statistics & Probability

☐ **How many soccer players have scored less than 4 goals?**

A   3   C   10

B   9   D   15

Common Core Standard 6.SP.A.4 – Statistics & Probability

☐ **How many soccer players have scored exactly 5 goals?**

A   0   C   5

B   3   D   6

Common Core Standard 6.SP.A.4 – Statistics & Probability

Salary per hour (in Dollars)

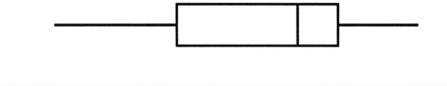

☐ **Look at the box plot above. What is the difference between highest and lowest salary per hour?**

A   2   C   4

B   3   D   9

Common Core Standard 6.SP.A.4 – Statistics & Probability

☐ **What is the interquartile range of the data in the box plot?**

A   2   C   4

B   3   D   9

Common Core Standard 6.SP.A.4 – Statistics & Probability

☐ **What is the median of the data in the box plot?**

A   24   C   28

B   27   D   30

Name_____

Common Core Standard 6.SP.B.5.A – Statistics & Probability

Number of books	0	1	2	3	4	5
Number of readers	3	6	5	3	2	1

Books read last month

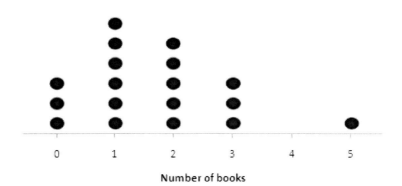

Number of books

☐ **Look at the data above. How many dots are missing in the empty column of a dot plot?**

A   1   C   3

B   2   D   4

Common Core Standard 6.SP.B.5.A – Statistics & Probability

☐ **How many people read books last month?**

A   5   C   15

B   6   D   17

Common Core Standard 6.SP.B.5.A – Statistics & Probability

☐ **How many people read 5 books?**

A   1   C   3

B   2   D   4

Name_____

Common Core Standard 6.SP.B.5.A – Statistics & Probability

Number of pet owners	0	1	2	3	4	5
Number of pets	6	8	5	3	1	2

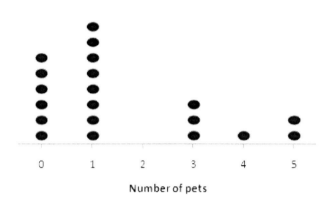

Pet owners

Number of pets

Look at the data above. How many dots are missing in the empty column of a dot plot?

A   3   C   6

B   5   D   8

Common Core Standard 6.SP.B.5.A – Statistics & Probability

How many owners have at least 3 pets?

A   3   C   6

B   4   D   8

Common Core Standard 6.SP.B.5.A – Statistics & Probability

How many owners have maximum number of pets?

A   2   C   6

B   5   D   8

Common Core Standard 6.SP.B.5.A – Statistics & Probability

Time bull riding (in minutes)	1	2	3	4	5
Number of bull riders	6	4	3	2	1

Bull riders

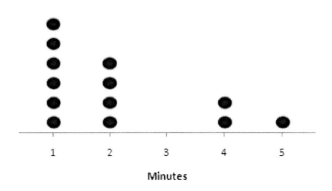

Minutes

☐ **Look at the data above. How many dots are missing in the empty column of a dot plot?**

A   1   C   3

B   2   D   4

Common Core Standard 6.SP.B.5.A – Statistics & Probability

☐ **How many bull riders were riding a bull for 2 minutes?**

A   1   C   4

B   2   D   6

Common Core Standard 6.SP.B.5.A – Statistics & Probability

☐ **How many bull riders were riding a bull?**

A   5   C   13

B   6   D   16

Name_____

Common Core Standard 6.SP.B.5.A – Statistics & Probability

Legs	2	4	6	8
Animals	5	9	7	4

Animals

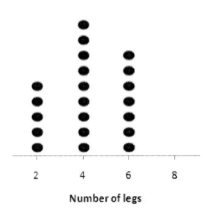

Number of legs

☐ **Look at the data above. How many dots are missing in the empty column of a dot plot?**

A   4   C   7

B   5   D   9

Common Core Standard 6.SP.B.5.A – Statistics & Probability

☐ **How many animals have 2 legs?**

A   4   C   7

B   5   D   9

Common Core Standard 6.SP.B.5.A – Statistics & Probability

☐ **How many animals were observed?**

A   8   C   21

B   9   D   25

Name_____

Common Core Standard 6.SP.B.5.A – Statistics & Probability

Trips to Europe	0	1	2	3	4
Number of trips		8	6	7	3

Trips to Europe

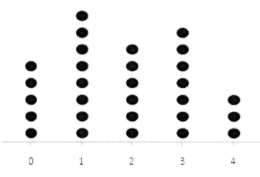

Number of trips

☐ **Look at the data above. Which number is missing in the empty cell of the table?**

A   5   C   7

B   6   D   8

Common Core Standard 6.SP.B.5.A – Statistics & Probability

☐ **How many people visited Europe only once?**

A   5   C   7

B   6   D   8

Common Core Standard 6.SP.B.5.A – Statistics & Probability

☐ **How many people visited Europe?**

A   4   C   24

B   8   D   29

Common Core Standard 6.SP.B.5.A – Statistics & Probability

Years of experience	0	1	2	3	4
Employees	5	3	8		6

Work experience

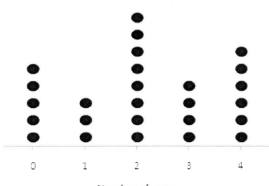

Number of years

☐ **Look at the data above. Which number is missing in the empty cell of the table?**

A   3   C   5

B   4   D   6

Common Core Standard 6.SP.B.5.A – Statistics & Probability

☐ **How many employees have no work experience?**

A   5   C   7

B   6   D   8

Common Core Standard 6.SP.B.5.A – Statistics & Probability

☐ **How many employees have work experience?**

A   14   C   21

B   17   D   26

Name_____

Common Core Standard 6.SP.B.5.A – Statistics & Probability

Number of foreign languages	0	1	2	3	4
Students	8	10		3	2

Students speaking foreign languages

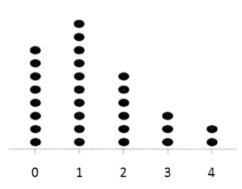

Number of foreign languages

☐ **Look at the data above. Which number is missing in the empty cell of the table?**

A   4   C   6

B   5   D   7

Common Core Standard 6.SP.B.5.A – Statistics & Probability

☐ **How many students speak 4 foreign languages?**

A   2   C   6

B   3   D   8

Common Core Standard 6.SP.B.5.A – Statistics & Probability

☐ **How many students were observed?**

A   4   C   21

B   10   D   29

Common Core Standard 6.SP.B.5.A – Statistics & Probability

Beds	1	2	3	4	5
Rooms	2		6	5	1

Rooms in the hotel

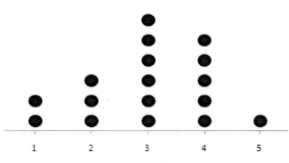

Number of beds

☐ **Look at the data above. Which number is missing in the empty cell of the table?**

A   1   C   5

B   3   D   6

Common Core Standard 6.SP.B.5.A – Statistics & Probability

☐ **How many rooms have 4 beds?**

A   2   C   4

B   3   D   5

Common Core Standard 6.SP.B.5.A – Statistics & Probability

☐ **How many rooms are there in the hotel?**

A   5   C   17

B   6   D   18

Name_____

Common Core Standard 6.SP.B.5.B – Statistics & Probability

Swimming in the Pool

Attempt	Time (sec)	Attempt	Time (sec)
1	15	5	19
2	18	6	34
3	12	7	27
4	25	8	20

☐ Look at the table above. What was the attribute measured?

A   Depth of the pool

B   Number of attempts

C   Length of time swimming in the pool

D   The dimensions of the pool

Common Core Standard 6.SP.B.5.B – Statistics & Probability

☐ What was the unit of measurement?

A   Seconds

B   Meters

C   Hours

D   Yards

Common Core Standard 6.SP.B.5.B – Statistics & Probability

☐ What was the number of observations?

A   8

B   15

C   20

D   34

Common Core Standard 6.SP.B.5.B – Statistics & Probability

Students Height (in cm)

185	168	173	182	191
174	193	157	165	163

☐ Look at the table above. What was the attribute measured?

A   Number of Students

B   Height

C   Wealth

D   Age

Common Core Standard 6.SP.B.5.B – Statistics & Probability

☐ What was the unit of measurement?

A   Seconds

B   Centimeters

C   Cubic meters

D   Light years

Common Core Standard 6.SP.B.5.B – Statistics & Probability

☐ What was the number of observations?

A   2

B   5

C   10

D   193

Common Core Standard 6.SP.B.5.B – Statistics & Probability

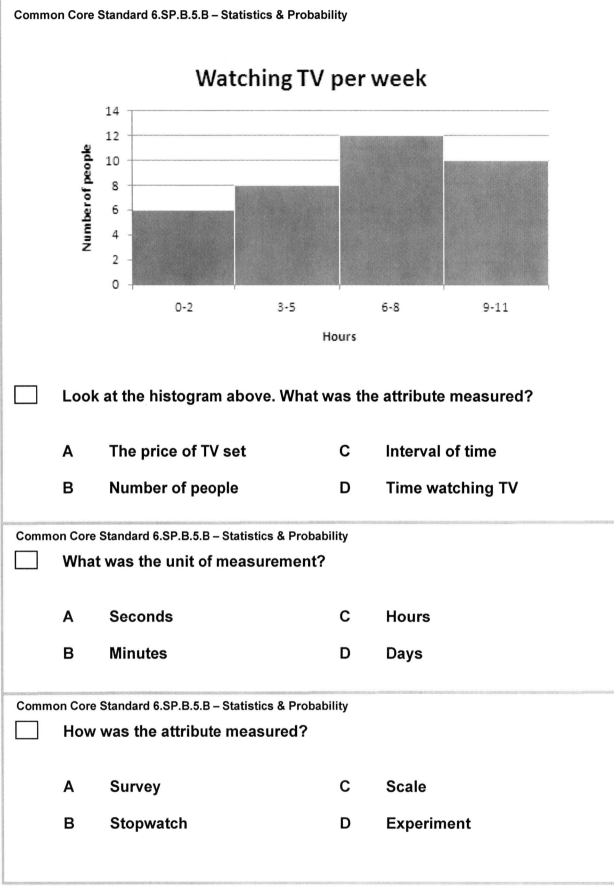

Watching TV per week

[ ] Look at the histogram above. What was the attribute measured?

A   The price of TV set   C   Interval of time

B   Number of people   D   Time watching TV

Common Core Standard 6.SP.B.5.B – Statistics & Probability

[ ] What was the unit of measurement?

A   Seconds   C   Hours

B   Minutes   D   Days

Common Core Standard 6.SP.B.5.B – Statistics & Probability

[ ] How was the attribute measured?

A   Survey   C   Scale

B   Stopwatch   D   Experiment

Common Core Standard 6.SP.B.5.B – Statistics & Probability

Workers' salaries per hour

| | $10 | $15 | $20 | $25 | $30 |

☐ **Look at the dot plot above. What was the attribute measured?**

A   **Number of workers**   C   **Salary per hour**

B   **The price of the company**   D   **Number of working hours**

Common Core Standard 6.SP.B.5.B – Statistics & Probability

☐ **What was the unit of measurement?**

A   **Dollars**   C   **Yards**

B   **Seconds**   D   **Pounds**

Common Core Standard 6.SP.B.5.B – Statistics & Probability

☐ **How was the attribute measured?**

A   **Stopwatch**   C   **Scale**

B   **Survey**   D   **Experiment**

Name_____

Common Core Standard 6.SP.B.5.B – Statistics & Probability

Car race

Lap	Time (sec)	Lap	Time (sec)
1	55	4	56
2	52	5	57
3	58	6	52

☐ **Look at the table above. What was the attribute measured?**

A   **Number of laps**

B   **Length of time driving a lap**

C   **Number of visitors**

D   **The price of the ticket**

Common Core Standard 6.SP.B.5.B – Statistics & Probability

☐ **What was the unit of measurement?**

A   **Seconds**

B   **Meters**

C   **Hours**

D   **Yards**

Common Core Standard 6.SP.B.5.B – Statistics & Probability

☐ **How was the attribute measured?**

A   **Scale**

B   **Stopwatch**

C   **Survey**

D   **Experiment**

Common Core Standard 6.SP.B.5.B – Statistics & Probability

Rabbits Weight (in pounds)

7	5	9	6	11	8
10	8	4	7	8	6

☐ Look at the table above. What was the attribute measured?

A Weight

B Height

C Wealth

D Age

Common Core Standard 6.SP.B.5.B – Statistics & Probability

☐ What was the unit of measurement?

A Kilograms

B Miles

C Pounds

D Meters

Common Core Standard 6.SP.B.5.B – Statistics & Probability

☐ How was the attribute measured?

A Experiment

B Stopwatch

C Survey

D Scale

Common Core Standard 6.SP.B.5.B – Statistics & Probability

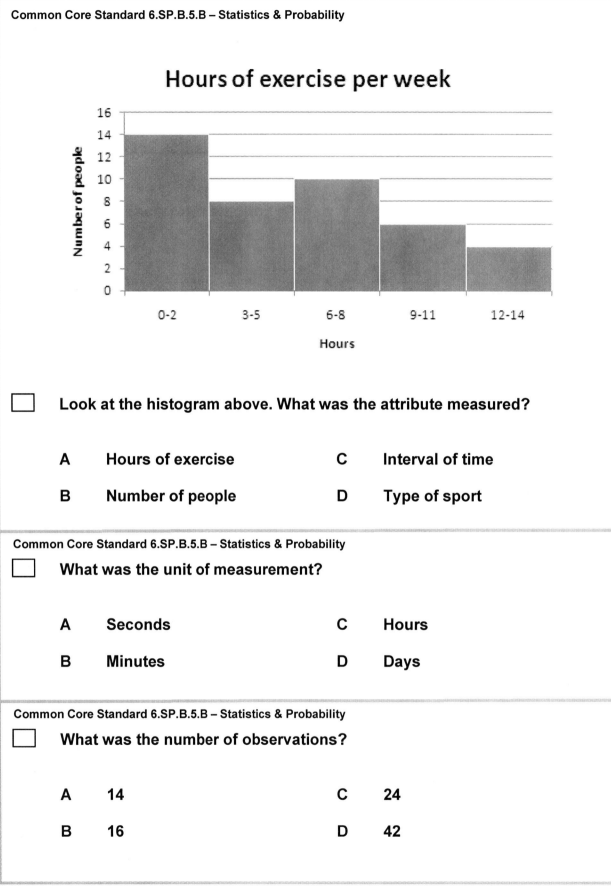

Hours of exercise per week

Look at the histogram above. What was the attribute measured?

A   Hours of exercise   C   Interval of time

B   Number of people   D   Type of sport

Common Core Standard 6.SP.B.5.B – Statistics & Probability

What was the unit of measurement?

A   Seconds   C   Hours

B   Minutes   D   Days

Common Core Standard 6.SP.B.5.B – Statistics & Probability

What was the number of observations?

A   14   C   24

B   16   D   42

Common Core Standard 6.SP.B.5.B – Statistics & Probability

Bouquet of Flowers

Number of bouquets

Number of flowers

☐   **Look at the dot plot above. What was the attribute measured?**

A   **Flowers in a bouquet**   C   **Price of a bouquet**

B   **Number of bouquets**   D   **Number of buyers**

Common Core Standard 6.SP.B.5.B – Statistics & Probability

☐   **What was the unit of measurement?**

A   **Buyers**   C   **Flowers**

B   **Shops**   D   **Bouquets**

Common Core Standard 6.SP.B.5.B – Statistics & Probability

☐   **What was the number of observations?**

A   **6**   C   **23**

B   **8**   D   **32**

Common Core Standard 6.SP.B.5.C – Statistics & Probability

Passengers on the Bus

Station	Passengers	Station	Passengers
1	24	5	25
2	22	6	25
3	24	7	27
4	20	8	25

☐ **Look at the table above. What is the mode?**

A   24

B   24.5

C   25

D   25.5

Common Core Standard 6.SP.B.5.C – Statistics & Probability

☐ **What is the median?**

A   24

B   24.5

C   25

D   25.5

Common Core Standard 6.SP.B.5.C – Statistics & Probability

☐ **What is the mean?**

A   24

B   24.5

C   25

D   25.5

Common Core Standard 6.SP.B.5.C – Statistics & Probability

Number of Floors in each Building

5	4	6	3	2	4
20	6	5	4	6	7

☐ **Look at the table above. What is the range?**

A   2

B   12

C   18

D   20

Common Core Standard 6.SP.B.5.C – Statistics & Probability

☐ **What is the interquartile range?**

A   2

B   2.5

C   3

D   3.5

Common Core Standard 6.SP.B.5.C – Statistics & Probability

☐ **What was the mean absolute deviation?**

A   2

B   2.5

C   3

D   3.5

Common Core Standard 6.SP.B.5.C – Statistics & Probability

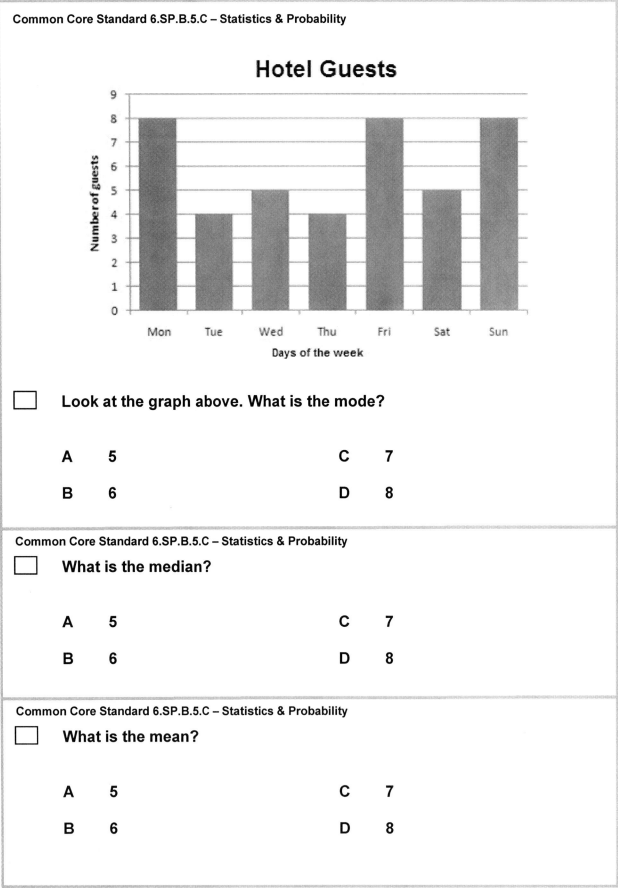

Hotel Guests

Look at the graph above. What is the mode?

A 5   C 7

B 6   D 8

Common Core Standard 6.SP.B.5.C – Statistics & Probability

What is the median?

A 5   C 7

B 6   D 8

Common Core Standard 6.SP.B.5.C – Statistics & Probability

What is the mean?

A 5   C 7

B 6   D 8

Common Core Standard 6.SP.B.5.C – Statistics & Probability

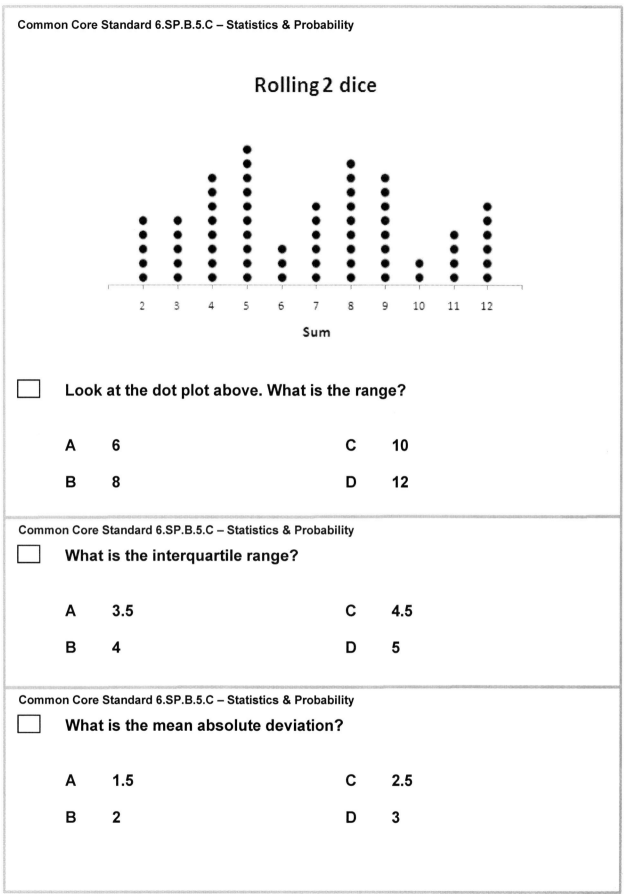

Rolling 2 dice

Sum

☐ **Look at the dot plot above. What is the range?**

A   6   C   10

B   8   D   12

Common Core Standard 6.SP.B.5.C – Statistics & Probability

☐ **What is the interquartile range?**

A   3.5   C   4.5

B   4   D   5

Common Core Standard 6.SP.B.5.C – Statistics & Probability

☐ **What is the mean absolute deviation?**

A   1.5   C   2.5

B   2   D   3

Common Core Standard 6.SP.B.5.C – Statistics & Probability

Number of Patients in ER Rooms

x, 3, 5, 2, 4, 1, 6, 4, 4, 1, 1, 1

☐ **Look at the data above. What must be the value of x so that data set is bimodal?**

A   1

B   2

C   3

D   4

Common Core Standard 6.SP.B.5.C – Statistics & Probability

☐ **What must be the value of x so that median is 2.5?**

A   2

B   3

C   4

D   5

Common Core Standard 6.SP.B.5.C – Statistics & Probability

☐ **What must be the value of x so that mean is 3.25?**

A   4

B   5

C   6

D   7

Common Core Standard 6.SP.B.5.C – Statistics & Probability

Shirt prices (in dollars)

18, 20, 16, 14, x, 23, 25

☐ Look at the data above. What must be the value of x so that the range is 15?

A   10

B   15

C   18

D   25

Common Core Standard 6.SP.B.5.C – Statistics & Probability

☐ What must be the value of x so that the interquartile range is 7?

A   10

B   12

C   14

D   16

Common Core Standard 6.SP.B.5.C – Statistics & Probability

☐ What must be the value of x so that the mean is 19?

A   8

B   17

C   12

D   14

Name_____

Common Core Standard 6.SP.B.5.C – Statistics & Probability

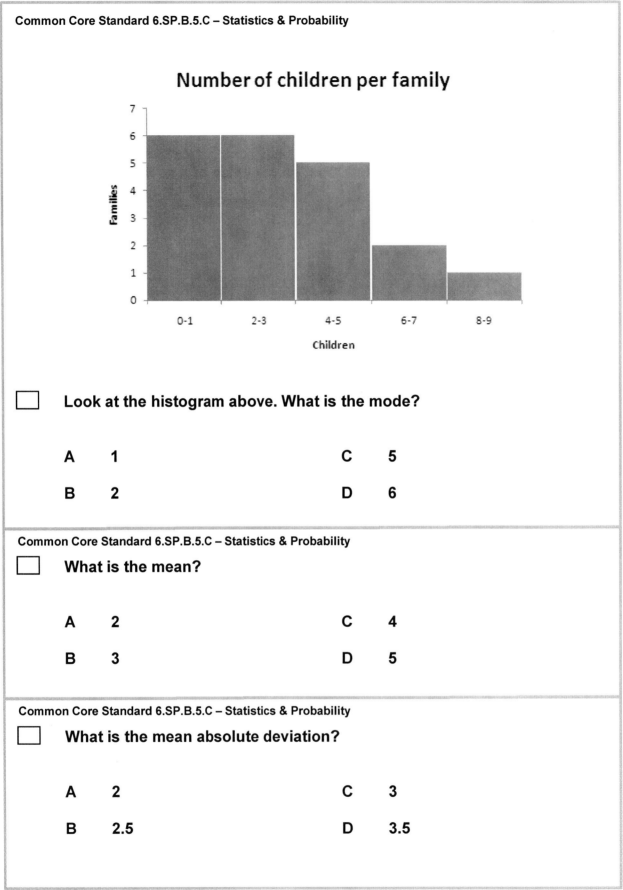

Number of children per family

Look at the histogram above. What is the mode?

A	1	C	5
B	2	D	6

Common Core Standard 6.SP.B.5.C – Statistics & Probability

What is the mean?

A	2	C	4
B	3	D	5

Common Core Standard 6.SP.B.5.C – Statistics & Probability

What is the mean absolute deviation?

A	2	C	3
B	2.5	D	3.5

Name_____

Common Core Standard 6.SP.B.5.C – Statistics & Probability

Poodle's Weight

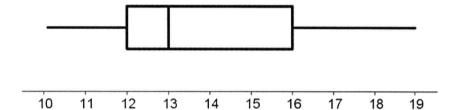

☐ **Look at the box plot above. What is the range?**

A   4   C   13

B   9   D   16

Common Core Standard 6.SP.B.5.C – Statistics & Probability

☐ **What is the interquartile range?**

A   4   C   13

B   12   D   16

Common Core Standard 6.SP.B.5.C – Statistics & Probability

☐ **What is the median?**

A   9   C   13

B   12   D   16

Name_____

Common Core Standard 6.SP.B.5.D – Statistics & Probability

Student	Age	Weight (kg)
Ishmail	7	40
Hannah	8	43
Ruben	7	36
Larissa	9	38
Keira	7	36
Morgan	16	44

☐   **Look at the age of students. What is the best measure of center?**

A   **Mean**

B   **Median**

C   **Mode**

D   **Range**

Common Core Standard 6.SP.B.5.D – Statistics & Probability

☐   **Look at the age of students. What is the best measure of variability?**

A   **Mean**

B   **Inter quartile range**

C   **Mode**

D   **Range**

Common Core Standard 6.SP.B.5.D – Statistics & Probability

☐   **Look at the weights of students. What is the best measure of center?**

A   **Mean**

B   **Median**

C   **Mode**

D   **Range**

Common Core Standard 6.SP.B.5.D – Statistics & Probability

Soccer player	Salary per week	Goals
Ryan	$3,000	1
Joseph	$4,000	3
Mallouk	$8,000	2
Alex	$9,000	6
Austin	$8,000	8
Dylan	$4,000	5
Armen	$9,000	12

☐ Look at the salaries of players. What is the best measure of center?

A   Mean

B   Median

C   Mode

D   Range

Common Core Standard 6.SP.B.5.D – Statistics & Probability

☐ Look at the salaries of players. What is the best measure of variability?

A   Mean

B   Inter quartile range

C   Mode

D   Range

Common Core Standard 6.SP.B.5.D – Statistics & Probability

☐ Look at the goals scored. What is the best measure of variability?

A   Mean

B   Median

C   Inter quartile range

D   Range

Common Core Standard 6.SP.B.5.D – Statistics & Probability

Employee	Hours Worked per Week	Absence (days)
Rachel	40	4
Jessica	10	3
Lydia	30	15
Mia	35	18
Molly	10	16
Amelia	10	13
Trinity	15	14

☐ Look at the working hours. What is the best measure of center?

A   Mean

B   Median

C   Mode

D   Range

Common Core Standard 6.SP.B.5.D – Statistics & Probability

☐ Look at the working hours. What is the best measure of variability?

A   Mean

B   Inter quartile range

C   Mode

D   Range

Common Core Standard 6.SP.B.5.D – Statistics & Probability

☐ Look at the days of absence. What is the best measure of center?

A   Mean

B   Median

C   Mode

D   Range

Name_____

Common Core Standard 6.SP.B.5.D – Statistics & Probability

Teacher	Years of experience	Number of subjects taught
Charles	40	2
Alexandra	12	1
Riley	15	3
Serena	4	1
Ian	8	2
Barbie	11	1

☐ Look at the years of experience. What is the best measure of center?

A   Mean

B   Median

C   Mode

D   Range

Common Core Standard 6.SP.B.5.D – Statistics & Probability

☐ Look at the years of experience. What is the best measure of variability?

A   Mean

B   Inter quartile range

C   Mode

D   Range

Common Core Standard 6.SP.B.5.D – Statistics & Probability

☐ Look at the days of absence. What is the best measure of variability?

A   Inter quartile range

B   Median

C   Mode

D   Range

Common Core Standard 6.SP.B.5.D – Statistics & Probability

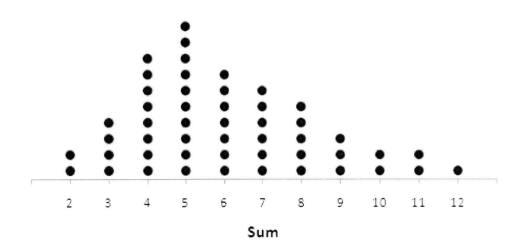

Look at the graph above. What is the best measure of center?

A   Mean   C   Mode

B   Range   D   Median

Common Core Standard 6.SP.B.5.D – Statistics & Probability

What is the best measure of variability?

A   Mean   C   Mode

B   Inter quartile range   D   Range

Common Core Standard 6.SP.B.5.D – Statistics & Probability

Which of the following is NOT a measure of center?

A   Mean   C   Range

B   Median   D   Mode

Name_____

Common Core Standard 6.SP.B.5.D – Statistics & Probability

Rolling dice

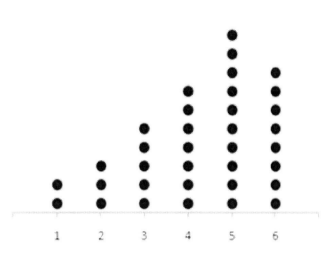

☐ Look at the graph above. What is the best measure of center?

A	Median	C	Range
B	Mode	D	Mean

Common Core Standard 6.SP.B.5.D – Statistics & Probability

☐ What is the best measure of variability?

A	Range	C	Inter quartile range
B	Mean	D	Mode

Common Core Standard 6.SP.B.5.D – Statistics & Probability

☐ Which of the following is NOT a measure of variability?

A	Inter quartile range	C	Range
B	Mean absolute deviation	D	Mode

Common Core Standard 6.SP.B.5.D – Statistics & Probability

Homework per Week

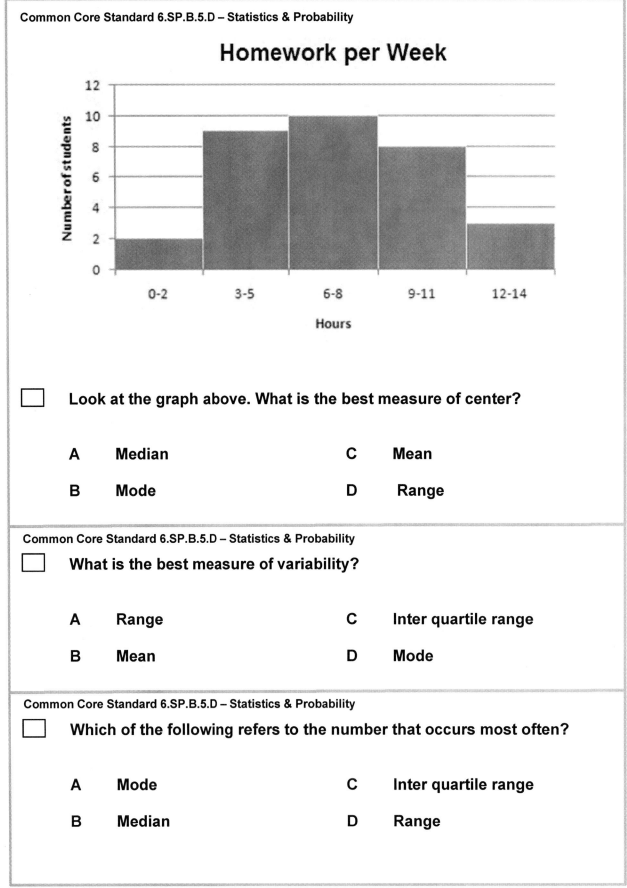

☐ **Look at the graph above. What is the best measure of center?**

A   Median   C   Mean

B   Mode   D   Range

Common Core Standard 6.SP.B.5.D – Statistics & Probability

☐ **What is the best measure of variability?**

A   Range   C   Inter quartile range

B   Mean   D   Mode

Common Core Standard 6.SP.B.5.D – Statistics & Probability

☐ **Which of the following refers to the number that occurs most often?**

A   Mode   C   Inter quartile range

B   Median   D   Range

Common Core Standard 6.SP.B.5.D – Statistics & Probability

Goals scored in a football game

1, 2, 6, 9, 7, 1, 0

☐ **What is the best measure of center?**

A   Mean

B   Mode

C   Median

D   Inter quartile range

Common Core Standard 6.SP.B.5.D – Statistics & Probability

☐ **What is the best measure of variability?**

A   Mean

B   Range

C   Mode

D   Inter quartile range

Common Core Standard 6.SP.B.5.D – Statistics & Probability

☐ **Which of the following is a measure of variability?**

A   Mean

B   Range

C   Mode

D   Median

ANSWER KEY

6.RP.A.1

Page 1 .... C, B, B

Page 2 .... C, A, D

Page 3 .... C, D, A

Page 4 .... B, D, C

Page 5 .... A, A, B

Page 6 .... C, B, D

Page 7 .... A, D, C

Page 8 .... B, D, A

6.RP.A.2

Page 9 .... A, B, C

Page 10 .... D, B, C

Page 11 .... C, D, B

Page 12 .... A, B, D

Page 13 .... B, D, C

Page 14 .... C, B, B

Page 15 .... B, C, D

Page 16 .... C, D, B

6.RP.A.3.A

Page 17 .... D, B, B

Page 18 .... A, C, A

Page 19 .... B, B, D

Page 20 .... D, C, A

Page 21 .... A, C, B

Page 22 .... D, C, A

Page 23 .... B, B, D

Page 24 .... C, D, D

6.RP.A.3.B

Page 25 .... C, B, D

Page 26 .... A, A, C

Page 27 .... C, D, B

Page 28 .... D, A, D

Page 29 .... B, A, C

Page 30 .... C, C, B

Page 31 .... D, B, C

Page 32 .... D, A ,B

6.RP.A.3.C

Page 33 .... C, C, B

Page 34 .... D, B, B

Page 35 .... C, D, B

Page 36 .... C, D, C

Page 37 .... A, B, B

Page 38 .... D, A, B

Page 39 .... B, C, D

Page 40 .... A, D, C

6.RP.A.3.D

Page 41 .... A, C, A

Page 42 .... B, B, D

Page 43 .... D, C, B

Page 44 .... C, A, C

Page 45 .... A, D, D

Page 46 .... A, B, C

Page 47 .... D, B, A

Page 48 .... D, B, B

6.NS.A.1

Page 49 .... D, A, C

Page 50 .... C, D, A

Page 51 .... C, A, D

Page 52 .... D, B, B

Page 53 .... C, B, C

Page 54 .... B, A, D

Page 55 .... D, C, D

Page 56 .... D, C, A

6.NS.B.2

Page 57 .... D, A, B

Page 58 .... D, B, C

Page 59 .... D, D, B

Page 60 .... C, B, A

Page 61 .... B, A, D

Page 62 .... D, B, C

Page 63 .... A, C, B

Page 64 .... C, B, D

6.NS.B.3

Page 65 .... A, D, B

Page 66 .... C, C, A

Page 67 .... A, B, D

Page 68 .... B, B, C

Page 69 .... D, A, A

Page 70 .... D, B, D

Page 71 .... A, C, D

Page 72 .... D, C, B

6.NS.B.4

Page 73 .... C, A, B

Page 74 .... C, D, C

Page 75 .... B, A, D

Page 76 .... A, C, D

Page 77 .... C, C, B

Page 78 .... A, A, C

Page 79 .... C, B, D

Page 80 .... D, A, B

6.NS.C.5

Page 81 .... D, B, D

Page 82 .... B, A, D

Page 83 .... D, A, B

Page 84 .... B, C, C

Page 85 .... D, B, C

Page 86 .... C, A, B

Page 87 .... A, D, C

Page 88 .... C, D, B

6.NS.C.6.A

Page 89 .... C, A, B

Page 90 .... D, A, C

Page 91 .... C, D, C

Page 92 .... B, D, B

Page 93 .... A, A, C

Page 94 .... B, C, C

Page 95 .... D, C, A

Page 96 .... B, A, C

6.NS.C.6.B

Page 97 .... A, B, D

Page 98 .... B, C, D

Page 99 .... C, A, B

Page 100 .... C, B, A

Page 101 .... B, D, D

Page 102 .... D, C, A

Page 103 .... A, B, D

Page 104 .... B, C, A

6.NS.C.6.C

Page 105 .... D, B, A

Page 106 .... B, D, A

Page 107 .... A, C, D

Page 108 .... C, D, A

Page 109 .... C, D, C

Page 110 .... B, B, A

Page 111 .... A, D, C

Page 112 .... C, D, C

6.NS.C.7.A

Page 113 .... D, C, A

Page 114 .... C, A, B

Page 115 .... D, D, B

Page 116 .... C, A, A

Page 117 .... D, C, B

Page 118 .... A, D, B

Page 119 .... A, C, B

Page 120 .... B, A, C

6.NS.C.7.B

Page 121 .... C, D, B

Page 122 .... A, C, B

Page 123 .... D, C, D

Page 124 .... A, D, B

Page 125 .... C, D, B

Page 126 .... B, D, D

Page 127 .... C, D, B

Page 128 .... C, A, D

6.NS.C.7.C

Page 129 .... D, A, D

Page 130 .... C, D, B

Page 131 .... D, C, A

Page 132 .... D, A, C

Page 133 .... A, C, D

Page 134 .... D, B, D

Page 135 .... C, B, C

Page 136 .... B, A, C

6.NS.C.7.D

Page 137 .... C, B, B

Page 138 .... D, B, A

Page 139 .... A, C, D

Page 140 .... D, B, D

Page 141 .... A, B, D

Page 142 .... D, D, C

Page 143 .... B, D ,C

Page 144 .... C, A, D

6.NS.C.8

Page 145 .... B, C, D

Page 146 .... C, B, A

Page 147 .... B, D, D

Page 148 .... C, A, D

Page 149 .... A, D, D

Page 150 .... B, A, C

Page 151 .... A, C, B

Page 152 .... B, C, B

6.EE.A.1

Page 153 .... A, C, D

Page 154 .... A, D, C

Page 155 .... B, C, C

Page 156 .... C, C, B

Page 157 .... C, A, B

Page 158 .... C, C, B

Page 159 .... B, C, A

Page 160 .... B, D, A

6.EE.A.2.A

Page 161 .... B, A, C

Page 162 .... D, A, B

Page 163 .... D, B, A

Page 164 .... C, A, B

Page 165 .... C, B, A

Page 166 .... C, A, B

Page 167 .... C, B, A

Page 168 .... D, A, A

6.EE.A.2.B

Page 169 .... A, B, C

Page 170 .... D, C, D

Page 171 .... B, D, A

Page 172 .... D, C, A

Page 173 .... D, A, D

Page 174 .... C, D, C

Page 175 .... D, B, A

Page 176 .... D, C, A

6.EE.A.2.C

Page 177 .... C, A, D

Page 178 .... B, A, D

Page 179 .... C, D, D

Page 180 .... D, D, C

Page 181 .... C, A, C

Page 182 .... B, C, C

Page 183 .... C, B, B

Page 184 .... C, A, B

6.EE.A.3

Page 185 .... C, D, A

Page 186 .... A, A, B

Page 187 .... C, D, D

Page 188 .... A, C, D

Page 189 .... D, A, B

Page 190 .... B, B, B

Page 191 .... A, D, D

Page 192 .... D, D, B

6.EE.A.4

Page 193 ………. D, B, A

Page 194 ………. B, D, C

Page 195 ………. D, C, A

Page 196 ………. A, D, C

Page 197 ………. C, B, A

Page 198 ………. D, C, A

Page 199 ………. D, C, B

Page 200 ………. C, D, A

6.EE.B.5

Page 201 ………. C, B, D

Page 202 ………. B, C, C

Page 203 ………. B, C, A

Page 204 ………. C, A, C

Page 205 ………. A, C, C

Page 206 ………. D, A, C

Page 207 ………. C, D, B

Page 208 ………. B, D, D

6.EE.B.6

Page 209 ………. C, B, A

Page 210 ………. D, A, B

Page 211 ………. A, D, B

Page 212 ………. C, B, A

Page 213 ………. B, B, A

Page 214 ………. C, D, A

Page 215 ………. D, B, A

Page 216 ………. C, D, A

6.EE.B.7

Page 217 ………. A, C, D

Page 218 ………. D, D, A

Page 219 ………. D, D, A

Page 220 ………. B, B, C

Page 221 ………. B, A, C

Page 222 ………. C, D, A

Page 223 ………. B, A, D

Page 224 ………. D, A, A

6.EE.B.8

Page 225 ………. B, A, D

Page 226 ………. C, B, A

Page 227 ………. C, B, D

Page 228 ………. A, D, B

Page 229 ………. A, C, D

Page 230 ………. C, C, C

Page 231 ………. C, A, D

Page 232 ………. C, A, B

6.EE.C.9

Page 233 ………. B, C, B

Page 234 ………. D, B, A

Page 235 ………. C, B, A

Page 236 ………. B, C, D

Page 237 ………. D, C, B

Page 238 ………. A, D, C

Page 239 ………. C, A, A

Page 240 ………. C, C, D

6.G.A.1

Page 241 .... C, A, C

Page 242 .... A, D, B

Page 243 .... B, B, C

Page 244 .... C, C, C

Page 245 .... A, A, D

Page 246 .... A, B, D

Page 247 .... C, B, A

Page 248 .... C, B, A

6.G.A.2

Page 249 .... A, D, B

Page 250 .... D, D, A

Page 251 .... A, C, D

Page 252 .... C, B, B

Page 253 .... A, C, B

Page 254 .... C, C, B

Page 255 .... A, C, C

Page 256 .... A, B, D

6.G.A.3

Page 257 .... D, D, A

Page 258 .... C, D, B

Page 259 .... C, B, B

Page 260 .... B, D, A

Page 261 .... C, B, A

Page 262 .... B, D, A

Page 263 .... C, B, C

Page 264 .... A, D, C

6.G.A.4

Page 265 .... B, D, C

Page 266 .... D, A, B

Page 267 .... C, B, D

Page 268 .... B, C, A

Page 269 .... B, C, A

Page 270 .... C, B, D

Page 271 .... C, A, C

Page 272 .... A, D, A

6.SP.A.1

Page 273 .... A, C, B

Page 274 .... B, C, A

Page 275 .... C, A, D

Page 276 .... D, B, A

Page 277 .... D, B, C

Page 278 .... A, D, C

Page 279 .... D, C, A

Page 280 .... C, D, A

6.SP.A.2

Page 281 .... B, D, A

Page 282 .... A, B, B

Page 283 .... C, C, A

Page 284 .... D, B, A

Page 285 .... C, B, B

Page 286 .... D, A, C

Page 287 .... B, C, C

Page 288 .... A, D, B

6.SP.A.3

Page 289 .... C, A, B

Page 290 .... C, D, B

Page 291 .... B, D, D

Page 292 .... B, C, D

Page 293 .... B, A, C

Page 294 .... B, C, C

Page 295 .... D, D, A

Page 296 .... C, D, A

6.SP.A.4

Page 297 .... C, D, B

Page 298 .... D, C, D

Page 299 .... C, B, C

Page 300 .... B, A, B

Page 301 .... C, A, D

Page 302 .... D, B, C

Page 303 .... B, B, A

Page 304 .... D, C, B

6.SP.A.5.A

Page 305 .... B, D, A

Page 306 .... B, C, A

Page 307 .... C, C, D

Page 308 .... A, B, D

Page 309 .... A, D, C

Page 310 .... B, A, C

Page 311 .... C, A, D

Page 312 .... B, D, C

6.SP.A.5.B

Page 313 .... C, A, A

Page 314 .... B, B, C

Page 315 .... D, C, A

Page 316 .... C, A, B

Page 317 .... B, A, B

Page 318 .... A, C, D

Page 319 .... A, C, D

Page 320 .... A, C, C

6.SP.A.5.C

Page 321 .... C, B, A

Page 322 .... C, A, B

Page 323 .... D, A, B

Page 324 .... B, B, B

Page 325 .... D, A, D

Page 326 .... A, D, B

Page 327 .... D, C, A

Page 328 .... B, A, C

6.SP.A.5.D

Page 329 .... B, B, A

Page 330 .... A, B, C

Page 331 .... A, B, B

Page 332 .... B, B, D

Page 333 .... D, B, C

Page 334 .... A, C, D

Page 335 .... C, C, A

Page 336 .... A, D, B

CPSIA information can be obtained at www.ICGtesting.com
Printed in the USA
BVOW04s0719070216

435840BV00005B/13/P